CULTURE SMART!
IRELAND

John Scotney

·K·U·P·E·R·A·R·D·

First published in Great Britain 2003
by Kuperard, an imprint of Bravo Ltd
59 Hutton Grove, London N12 8DS
Tel: +44 (0) 20 8446 2440 Fax: +44 (0) 20 8446 2441
www.culturesmartguides.com
Inquiries: sales@kuperard.co.uk

Culture Smart!® is a registered trademark of Bravo Ltd

Distributed in the United States and Canada
by Random House Distribution Services
1745 Broadway, New York, NY 10019
Tel: +1 (212) 572-2844 Fax: +1 (212) 572-4961
Inquiries: csorders@randomhouse.com

Series Editor Geoffrey Chesler
Design Bobby Birchall

ISBN 978 1 85733 308 4

British Library Cataloguing in Publication Data
A CIP catalogue entry for this book is available from the
British Library

Printed in Malaysia

Cover image: Bantry Bay, County Cork.
Travel Ink/Angela Hampton

About the Author

JOHN SCOTNEY is an Anglo-Irish writer, producer, teacher, and broadcaster. He was the BBC's Head of Drama in Ireland and later Head of BBCTV Drama Script Unit. He has written books and articles about literature and the media, and written and directed numerous programs for the BBC, many on Irish themes. He is a former Chair of the Writers' Guild of Great Britain, Deputy Chair of the National Poetry Society, and a Fellow of the Royal Society of Arts.

The Culture Smart! series is continuing to expand.
For further information and latest titles visit
www.culturesmartguides.com

The publishers would like to thank **CultureSmart!**Consulting for its help in researching and developing the concept for this series.

CultureSmart!Consulting creates tailor-made seminars and consultancy programs to meet a wide range of corporate, public-sector, and individual needs. Whether delivering courses on multicultural team building in the USA, preparing Chinese engineers for a posting in Europe, training call-center staff in India, or raising the awareness of police forces to the needs of diverse ethnic communities, it provides essential, practical, and powerful skills worldwide to an increasingly international workforce.

For details, visit www.culturesmartconsulting.com

CultureSmart!Consulting and **CultureSmart!** guides have both contributed to and featured regularly in the weekly travel program "Fast Track" on BBC World TV.

contents

contents

Map of Ireland

NORTH CHANNEL

NORTHEN IRELAND

LONDONDERRY

Londonderry

LONDON-
DERRY

ANTRIM

DONEGAL

Omagh

TYRONE

Belfast

Armagh

DOWN

FERMANAGH

ARMAGH

Sligo

MONAGHAN

SLIGO

LEITRIM

CAVAN

MAYO

ROSCOMMON

LONGFORD

LOUTH

MEATH

DUBLIN

GALWAY

WESTMEATH

Dublin

Galway

OFFALY

KILDARE

ATLANTIC
OCEAN

LAOIS

WICKLOW

CLARE

CARLOW

Limerick

TIPPERARY

KILKENNY

WEXFORD

LIMERICK

Tipperary

Wexford

Tralee

Killarney

CORK

WATERFORD

Waterford

IRISH
SEA

KERRY

Cork

REPUBLIC OF IRELAND

introduction

This is a book about Ireland and its people, not
"the Irish" in the broadest sense. Visitors from the
crowded cities of America, from densely
populated mainland Europe, and from even more
densely populated Japan are often delighted by
how empty Ireland seems, with its broad
countryside, little towns, and uncongested roads.
Northern Ireland is three times as densely peopled
as the Republic, yet even so the whole island is
home to only about five and a half million people.

But as for "the Irish" worldwide—that is a
different matter!

There are forty million citizens in the U.S.A. of
Irish descent, and ten American presidents were of
Irish stock, including Presidents Kennedy, Nixon,
Reagan, and Clinton. 15 percent of the population of
New Zealand and 30 percent of Australians have Irish
forebears. Ned Kelly came from an Irish immigrant
family, as did all his gang, and the policeman whom
he shot. Even in the 1860s, 20 percent of Canadians
were descended from former Irish immigrants.

Argentina has an ethnic Irish population of
around 300,000, and Irishmen played major roles
in the development of South America. Bernard
O'Higgins, Captain General of Chile, Grand
Marshal, and Captain General of Peru, General of
Grand Colombia etc., etc., is counted among the
Libertadores, the heroes of South America's

struggle for independence. As for Britain—in Britain there are up to a million people born in Ireland, and perhaps five million of Irish descent.

What this colossal exodus means to the Irish, how it came about, and how the population of Ireland fell from eight million in 1840, is something you will need to know if you are to understand modern Ireland. But there are many other things worth knowing about this remarkable island that has peopled so much of the world with men and women who still remain loyal to their origins, and that has given the world so much in the way of music, poetry, drama, and literature in general. This little land has had an influence and indeed endured a history out of all proportion to its size, and it has done so because of its people.

Most guidebooks tell you where to stay and what to see. This series is written for people who want to know more and go deeper. Here you will find the beliefs and attitudes of the Irish, their rich musical and literary culture, their ancient language and mythology, the values they live by, how they do business, how they enjoy themselves, the way they have been molded by their history and indeed by geography. This understanding will be appreciated by your hosts; it will open doors to you, even open the hearts of a generous, talented people, justifiably proud of their unique identity.

Key Facts – The Republic of Ireland

Ireland is a single geographical entity—an island off the western coast of Europe. It is home to two political units, one an independent self-governing republic, Eire (pronounced "AIR-uh'"), often called "the Republic," to distinguish it from Northern Ireland, which is part of the United Kingdom with some elements of self-government.

Official Name	Eire, or Ireland	Article 4 of the Republic's 1937 constitution states "The name of the state is Eire or in the English language, Ireland."
Capital city	Dublin	
Main cities	Dublin, Cork, Galway, Limerick	
Area	About 27,000 square miles (70,000 square kilometers). Eire occupies 85% of the island of Ireland, all except the northeastern corner.	
Climate	Temperate	
Population	About 3.7 million. Nearly a million in Dublin. 40% of population live within 50 miles (100 kilometers) of Dublin. Over 25% of population are under fourteen, and 41% under twenty-five. Growth rate: 1% + per annum.	
Currency	The Euro	
Ethnic Mix	Over 99% native Irish. Small Jewish, Indian and Chinese minorities.	
Family Size	Av. family size 2.11	Av. no. of children per woman 1.9
Language	Two official languages: Gaelic and English. Gaelic is studied in schools, but is spoken fluently by only 100,000 people (who also speak English). Many Gaelic words appear in public life.	

Religion	90% Roman Catholic. The rest mainly Anglican.	
Government	Parliament, called the *Oireachtas*, has two chambers: the Senate, *Seanad Eireann*, and the house of representatives, the *Dail Eireann*. The head of state is the President, elected for seven years. Real power lies with the *Taioseach*, or Prime Minister.	
Local Government Structure	Eire is divided into 26 counties. Ancient Ireland was made up of four provinces, formerly kingdoms: Ulster, Munster, Leinster, and Connaught. Ulster is now almost wholly in Northern Ireland.	
Legal System	The heads of the legal system are the judges of the Supreme Court, appointed by the President on the advice of the Prime Minister and cabinet. The legal system is based on English Common Law, but much modified by the Constitution and by laws and judgments made since independence.	
Cost of Living	Consumer spending is constantly rising, but the cost of living remains lower than in the United Kingdom.	
Ports and Airports	Dublin and Cork are the main ports, Dublin and Shannon the main airports.	
Media	Publicly funded TV & Radio (RTE, *Radio Telefis Eirann*) has two English television channels: RTE1 and Network 2, and an Irish-language channel, TG4. The independent commercial station is TV3. All carry commercials.	There are 3 English-language RTE radio networks: Radio 1, Radio 2, and the classical music station Lyric FM; plus Radio Ireland, the Irish-language *Radio na Gaeltachta*, and numerous local stations.
	Several English-language newspapers, notably the *Irish Times*, are also available daily on the Web.	

Electricity	The Irish electrical system operates on 220 volts/ 50 cycles.	Sockets and plugs are the same as in the U.K. Visitors from continental Europe will need adapters. Americans will need adapters both for the voltage cycles and plugs and sockets.
Telephone	The international code for Ireland is 00 353.	The Irish telecommunications system is one of the most advanced in Europe.
Time	Ireland is on Greenwich Mean time. Times are the same as for the United Kingdom.	

Key Facts – Northern Ireland

Official Name	Province of Northern Ireland	The Province is sometimes called Ulster, but actually includes only six of the original nine counties of Ulster.
Capital	Belfast	
Main cities	Belfast, Londonderry, Omagh	
Area	5,500 square miles (14,000 square kilometers)	
Climate	Temperate	
Population	1.6 million. Mostly in the east, where Belfast has a population of nearly 300,000.	

Currency	Pound Sterling. English notes and coins are legal tender, as are the notes issued by Scottish banks. Additionally two Northern Irish banks issue their own notes.
Ethnic Mix	99% Northern Irish, many with Scottish forebears. Small Indian and larger Chinese communities.
Family size	Family size: 2.1
Language	English
Religion	60% Protestant, 40% Catholic
Government	Northern Ireland is part of the United Kingdom and elects 17 members to the British Parliament, but has its own Assembly at Stormont.
Legal System	As in the U.K., with some modifications, notably under the Prevention of Terrorism Act 1974.
Cost of Living	Noticeably lower than elsewhere in the U.K.
Media	Northern Ireland has BBC radio and TV channels plus the commercial Ulster Television.
Ports and Airports	Belfast is one of the U.K.'s major ports. The International airport is about 20 miles from Belfast, but there is also a small airport within the city.
Electricity	Northern Ireland is on 240 volts, as in the rest of the United Kingdom.
Telephone	The international code for Northern Ireland is 00 44, the same as for the United Kingdom.
Time	Greenwich Mean Time, plus one hour forward in summer. Northern Ireland is in the same time zone as the United Kingdom and Eire.

chapter one

LAND &
PEOPLE

GEOGRAPHY AND CLIMATE

Set at the very edge of Europe, battered by the Atlantic but warmed by the Gulf Stream, Ireland is tethered a few miles off the coasts of Wales, England, and Scotland. But in its shape—the smooth east coast and the straggling indented west coast—it seems to be reaching out across the Atlantic Ocean toward America, where so many of its sons and daughters now live.

Not just Ireland's position, but the nature of the land itself has shaped the way of life of the people and their attitudes toward themselves and others.

Ireland is famous for its greenness, and this greenness has become part of the Irish national identity: the national flag is green, white, and orange; the sportsmen and women play in green; even the telephone boxes are green.

Connemara on the west coast, which faces the great ocean head on, is not green. It is a brown, rugged, and bleak place of stones and of few trees. Yet it has a great natural grandeur and it is here that the old ways are best preserved. Otherwise

Ireland indeed has a largely green, gentle landscape, and what are called mountains here would be called hills elsewhere.

The Donegal Highlands in the northeast rise to about 700 feet (about 230 meters), but even Slieve Donard, the highest peak of the Mountains of Mourne, sweeps down to the sea from a height of just 2,786 feet (849 meters). The Wicklow Mountains in the east rise to a similar height. In the south the wonderfully named Macgillycuddy's Reeks are a little higher, making them the highest mountains in the whole island.

Ireland is a place of hills and planes, but above all it is a land of rivers and lakes; the Republic alone has 537 square miles (1,390 square kilometers) of water. Most people have heard of the beautiful

Lakes of Killarney, but few realize Lough Neagh in Ulster is the largest lake in the British Isles. All this water is put to good use, being harnessed to generate enough hydroelectricity to provide many of Ireland's citizens with power.

The "pleasant waters of the river Lee," the Blackwater, the Suir, the Nore, the Barrow, the Liffey, from whose water Guinness is supposed to be made, the Boyne where a famous battle was fought, and the Lagan on which the city of Belfast stands, all flow toward the east. Only the Bann flows north; and the Shannon, two hundred fifty miles long and the longest river in the British Isles, flows south.

The Shannon divides the rich green pastures of the east from the bleakness of Connaught (or Connacht). Oliver Cromwell is said to have sworn to drive the rebel Irish "to Hell or Connaught" as two equally insalubrious places. To the north of the Shannon lies the lovely county of Clare, with the unique landscape of the rocky Burren country.

Galway, in its famous bay, is the major city of the west and looks to the sea rather than the land.

No rivers flow into the sea in Connaught, but there is no shortage of water. The west is often seen as the most distinctively Irish part of the country—it is certainly the wettest. The water-bearing clouds fresh from the Atlantic strike the rising ground and the rain comes down in bucketfuls. But there's still plenty left for the rest of the country.

For Ireland's greenness comes from its climate which, to be honest, does involve a certain amount of rain. Even the driest parts around Dublin get 150 days of rain a year, and an annual total of 29.5 inches (75 cm) of rainfall. Bring your umbrellas and waterproof gear even in the sunniest months of May and June, but be prepared equally for beautiful sunny days in February or November. The skies are often overcast, but the sun is always ready to surprise you by showing her face when she is least expected—the sun is a female noun in Irish, and was once a goddess. The combination of sunshine and moisture makes for wonderful sunsets over Galway Bay and for glorious rainbows. And all you have to do is find the foot of a rainbow to claim a Leprechaun's crock of gold.

If an Irishman tells you it's "a grand soft day" that will mean it is raining gently but the day is quite pleasantly warm. For the climate is surprisingly mild, milder than might be expected at such a northern latitude thanks to the warm seas of the Gulf Stream that wash Ireland's shores. The rain rarely turns to snow, and temperatures in the east range from about 39°F (4°C) in January to 68°F (20°C) in August.

The mild but wet climate affects many aspects of Irish culture. The ancient Irish clans roamed widely to rustle each other's cattle, and epic poems like *The Cattle Raid of Cooley* were recited about their deeds. These heroes never settled down to become respectable farmers tilling fields of wheat because wheat does not grow well in this climate. The rainfall is wonderful for grass, but wheat tends to rot. Even today 68 percent of the agricultural land of the Republic is under permanent pasture and only 13 percent is arable.

The northernmost county is Donegal, distinctively beautiful and with magnificent beaches. Just south of Donegal, Sligo was immortalized by the poems of W. B. Yeats.

About a third of Ireland is made up of a central plain covered with clay, deposited when the ice sheets withdrew at the end of the last ice age, which retains a lot of surface water from the copious rainfall. Here peat moss thrives and over thousands of years has built up into peat bogs, a sort of embryonic coal—though the island has very little true coal. Most of the bogs have been drained so the peat can be cut for fuel. The scent of a peat fire (the Irish often call peat "turf") drifting from a cottage chimney is unforgettable.

Ireland is known for the excellence of its beef and dairy products. The green pastures of the central plain are devoted mainly to dairying, but also raise fine pigs, and the wonderful grass of the Curragh breeds famous horses. Beef cattle from the west are sent eastward to the richer pastures of Meath for fattening. James Joyce writes in *Ulysses* of a young woman being "beef to the heels like in Mullingar Heifer." There are few golden fields of corn; instead oats and potatoes are grown, and in the comparatively dry sunny southeast, barley—

Cork is famous for its brewing and distilling.

West of the west coast are the Aran Islands. These rocky places, battered by the seas and gales of the Atlantic, have an emotional significance to Irish people out of all proportion to the number of their inhabitants.

People have lived on Aran for 4,000 years, and the islands are a treasure house of antiquities and Celtic remains. Gaelic is still some people's first language, though English is today heard almost as often. Here the old traditions and folklore lasted longer than on the mainland. The way of life was hard. Seaweed and sand were carried from the shore to cover the barren rocks with some sort of soil, which had to be held in by stone walls to keep it from being blown back into the sea. The tiny fields supported at best a single cow or a few scraggy sheep. To catch fish the islanders would brave the Atlantic rollers in *currachs*—frail canvas boats that they rowed with remarkable courage and skill.

Nowadays the island economy is rather more prosperous. In the course of the summer season 100,000 visitors arrive, and many of them take away with them one of the famous Aran sweaters (or *ganseys*) knitted in complex and individual Celtic designs.

Don't Overdo It!

Many visitors like to stock up on distinctive Irish clothing—Aran sweaters, tweeds, and the like. By all means wear them while in the country but be careful not to overdo it; a visitor who wears a lot of traditional clothing might be the subject of a certain sly humor.

Northern Ireland, which comprises only about a sixth of the island, contains about 30 percent of its population and is generally more industrialized, though mainly in the east, and it is easy to escape into areas of real peace.

Its physical geography differs little from the rest of Ireland. You will sometimes hear the north called "Ulster" though this is not strictly correct—

the old kingdom of Ulster also included three counties that are part of the Republic.

The weather is no less rainy than that of the Republic, and the winters are equally mild.

Old Ulsterman: *If you can see Carickfergus Castle on the opposite side of Belfast Lough that means its going to rain.*
Visitor: *And if you can't see it?*
Old Ulsterman: *That means it's already raining.*

The damp climate and pure water were well suited to the cultivation and preparation of flax, and Northern Ireland is world famous for its linen.

Finally, Ireland is the best place to be on the planet if you want to avoid earthquakes. No epicenter has ever been found anywhere on the entire island!

IRISH SOCIETY AND PEOPLE

The pattern of life in Ireland has come to resemble that of its neighbors. Superficially, it can be hard to tell an English, Scots, or Welsh person from someone from Ireland. People dress the same, speak the same language, have many of the same tastes as those in mainland Britain.

This has not always been so and underneath the surface there are significant differences. Many of these differences are born out of historical experience. To understand the Irish you must be aware of the events that have shaped and still shape their thoughts and feelings. Ireland is a complex place where the apparent similarity to other Western countries can be misleading. A little trouble taken to learn its customs, etiquette, and traditions will be amply rewarded.

The English are famously ignorant of Irish history—if they had understood it a bit better their attitude might have been, and might still be, different. On the other hand, the Irish are steeped in their history, both real and mythical. Their history and their religion have forged the national consciousness—which is why, throughout this book, you will find plenty of snippets of history.

For nearly eight hundred years England ruled Ireland. For much of that time effective English government could only be imposed within fifty miles of Dublin, the so-called Pale of Dublin—those outside English control being considered barbarians and so "beyond the Pale." But at other times English rule extended throughout the island and was often harsh, repressive, and bitterly resented.

An Open Society

If yesterday the English were the ruling class and the Irish were the ruled, today the most obvious characteristic of Irish society is its openness and lack of any obvious class structure. Everybody uses first names except, significantly, priests and nuns, who are always Father this or Sister that. The Anglo-Irish, once the landowning gentry, still exist, but are tolerated rather than revered—especially since Irish farmers are no longer tenants but own their land.

Ireland scarcely experienced the Victorian industrialization that created the working-class/middle-class division in English society, except to some extent in what is now Northern Ireland, and there the fiercely egalitarian nature of the dominant Presbyterian Church militated against obvious class differences.

The result is that Irish society is fairly heterogeneous, with most people having similar roots in rural culture. To suggest that there is absolutely no distinctive Irish working-class culture is an exaggeration—as witness the plays of Sean O'Casey and, more recently, the novels of Roddy Doyle. Another famous writer, Brendan Behan, was proud of being the working-class son of a Dublin painter and decorator. Yet his mother's family came from a family of farmers in County Meath, while his mother's brother, the poet Paedar Kearney, actually wrote the Irish national anthem, "The Soldiers' Song."

Nevertheless, given Dublin's size, a rural/urban divide is inevitable. Dublin in the new millennium is awash with new money as successful entrepreneurs and entertainers pay lavish sums for the houses of the old English rulers. "Dublin 4," actually refers to a postal area, but the term is used to sum up the cosmopolitan prejudices (as opposed to sturdy rural values!) of the urban elite who live there. Then there are the so-called "chattering classes": intellectuals, politicians, bureaucrats, and professionals found in certain southside Dublin pubs. Country-dwellers can feel misunderstood and maligned by such people, and tend to distrust them, though less so as prosperity percolates throughout the country.

In the countryside, social life is being reinvigorated by a number of factors, including tourism. About one-seventh of the labor force is involved in farming—much higher than the European Union average but a long way removed from the idealistic view of Ireland expressed by President Eamon de Valera in his 1943 St. Patrick's Day broadcast:

> *"A land whose countryside would be bright with cosy homesteads, whose fields and villages would be . . . joyous with the romping of sturdy children,*

the contests of athletic youths and the laughter of comely maidens . . . "

There is a lively interest in genealogical matters, and not just from expatriate families. Heredity is important, especially in politics and the professions of law and medicine, whose members are at least as conservative as their counterparts elsewhere. Although Eire does not grant aristocratic titles it does have a Chief Herald whose office grants coats of arms, and there are several organizations that can help you trace your Irish roots.

Status

However, by and large those people perceived to be at the top of Irish society come from the new class of entrepreneurs, some of whom are extremely wealthy by any international yardstick. Status is generally derived either from wealth or talent. What people achieve is determined by their own efforts rather than by background and education.

The Irish revere their dead heroes, but toward the living they are more likely to show decent respect than reverence. Irish culture is naturally artistic, particularly in the arts of poetry and drama, but those who excel in these fields are seen as part of society, not some sort of elite.

Irish Irreverence

In England the eminent poet Seamus Heaney, Professor of Poetry at Oxford University, was offered the title of Poet Laureate, which as a republican he refused. In Ireland the traditional irreverent populism is a great leveler, and he is gently mocked as "Famous Seamus." He is respected and admired, but not put on a pedestal.

Tax Free Art

Artists, especially writers, are attracted to Ireland by a taxation system that allows the income from artistic activity to be tax free. The presence of so many artists from around the world has been a major influence on society over the last quarter-century.

THE IMPORTANCE OF HISTORY TO THE IRISH

There is probably no country in the world where the attitudes and values of its modern inhabitants are so much the product of their history. Certain key events or concepts have become part of the Irish mind-set. You will hear people speaking of the "Island of Saints and Scholars," and quite probably references to the "Flight of the Earls," "the Plantation of Ulster," the "Curse of

Cromwell," "the Penal Laws," "the Protestant Ascendancy," "the 98," Robert Emmet's speech from the dock, and "O'Connell and Catholic Emancipation." Northern Protestants will tell you about "the Apprentice Boys of Derry" and "King Billy and the Battle of the Boyne." And all spoken of as if they were still living issues—as to many Irish people they are!

Land of Saints and Scholars

Ireland has been inhabited since about 7,000–8,000 BCE when the first colonists arrived from Scotland, which was probably linked to Ireland by land. The Neolithic or Stone Age inhabitants who constructed massive religious monuments such as the megalithic tomb at New-Grange (within easy driving distance of Dublin and well worth a visit) began to arrive by boat from Britain some 4,000 years later.

The sixth century BCE brought the Celts, who ushered in a dynamic era of early civilization. Ireland rejoices in the largest collection of prehistoric gold artifacts found in Western Europe; you can see them at the National Museum in Dublin.

Every Irishman knows that what sets Ireland apart from most of Europe is the fact that it was never part of the Roman Empire, at a time when most of mainland Britain had submitted to the

Roman yoke. In fact the Romans were not interested in occupying a country that had no metals of its own, and could not grow the grain needed to feed their armies.

Greco-Roman classical learning and literacy came to Ireland with the introduction of Christianity and writing in the fifth century. Latin civilization fused with the Celtic decorative tradition to produce such masterpieces as the wonderful Ardagh Chalice, the Book of Durrow, and the Book of Kells.

Sometimes the monks grew bored with the slow, painstaking copying of the Gospels, and scribbled short lyrics in the margins of their work, like this, written in an eighth-century copy of St. Paul's Epistles.

"I and Pangur Ban, my cat,
'Tis a like task we are at;
Hunting mice is his delight,
Hunting words I sit all night . . .

Better far than praise of men
'Tis to sit with book and pen . . . "

Extract from *Pangur Ban*, trans. Robin Flower

Among the hundreds of monasteries founded were the great centers of Clonmacnoise in County Offaly, and Monastarboice in County Louth. This was a golden age for Ireland, which became a refuge for classical scholarship and Christian learning in a Europe that was elsewhere sinking back into barbarity. Hence the pride in being the "Island of Saints and Scholars"!

The Vikings and St. Brendan

The Viking invasions from the ninth century onward brought death and destruction but also

trade, currency, and the foundation of most of the major towns including Dublin. It was in the ninth century that *The Voyage of St. Brendan* was written, which seems to describe a journey across the Atlantic to America by the Irish saint.

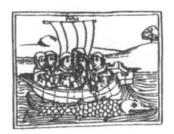

Tara and the High Kings

All this time Ireland was divided into separate kingdoms. There were "High Kings" (*Ard-Ri* in Gaelic) based at the hill of Tara in County Meath, with a great hall 700 feet (240 meters) long, but their title was honorary and sacred, and they wielded no real power over other rulers. Yet these various kingdoms shared a language, a set of laws, the Brehon Laws, and a common artistic, literary, and musical culture. As early as the third century CE the High King, Cormac, founded what was in effect a royal academy to promote poetry and the law.

In 1014 the High King Brian Boru defeated the Norsemen at the Battle of Clontarf—typically he was also fighting other Irishmen, the men of Leinster having sided with the Vikings!

The Normans

An Anglo-Norman adventurer, the Earl of Pembroke, known as Strongbow, arrived in 1170, invited across by an Irish king who was quarreling with the High King. The mounted and mailed Norman knights with their big horses, lances, archers (the Irish only had slings), and impregnable castles were in a different class from the *kernes*, the Irish foot soldiers. They soon controlled all of Ireland except for part of Ulster, and for the first time Ireland was theoretically part of the kingdom of England.

Very little of the island actually came under direct English rule. Most of the local Norman and native Irish chiefs were a law unto themselves, and the King of England's writ only ran in the Pale, which extended about fifty miles from Dublin.

More Irish than the Irish!

The Norman barons intermarried with the Irish, adopted Irish ways and laws, and even learned to speak Gaelic, so that Norman surnames like Fitzgerald, Costello, or Butler, now seem as Irish as O'Connor or O'Brian. Indeed they were accused of being *Hibernicis ipsis Hibernior*— "More Irish than the Irish." Be warned: the visitor who tries too zealously to copy Irish ways is often today ridiculed as "More Irish than the Irish."

The Flight of the Earls and the Plantation of Ulster

Only in the Tudor era of the sixteenth century was Ireland beyond the Pale brought anything like under control. This century also saw the start of the great religious divide between Protestants and Catholics, since the introduction of the Elizabethan prayer book was the first serious attempt to impose the Protestant Reformation on the Irish people. In Tudor times Ulster in the North was the heartland of the native Irish. Its great chieftain, Hugh O'Neill, Earl of Tyrone, was brought up in Queen Elizabeth's court. Yet when England was at war with Spain he and his powerful neighbor, Hugh O'Donnell, marched their men all the way to the south to try to rescue a Spanish force besieged in Kinsale. They were routed.

O'Neill was pardoned in 1603, but hated to serve where he had ruled. In 1607 he and the Earl of Tyrconnell, Hugh O'Donnell's son, fled to France and then Rome. The "Flight of the Earls" was followed by the dispossession of many Catholics in Ulster, and their lands were given to Englishmen and, especially, Scots—the two realms having just been united under James I of England (and VI of Scotland).

These colonists would be hated by the Irish they displaced and would support the Crown. This was the "Plantation of Ulster," and it explains why so many people in Ulster have Scottish names, are Presbyterians like the Scots, and are still loyal to the British Crown.

The Curse of Cromwell

In 1641, just before the English Civil War, the Irish rebelled and the question of who should control the forces sent against them actually precipitated the war. During the war they theoretically sided with the King and in consequence were savagely suppressed by Oliver Cromwell, the Lord Protector and leader of the victorious Parliamentary forces. The massacres following the sieges of Drogheda and Wexford in 1649 have made Cromwell a name loathed in the south; to put the "Curse of Cromwell" on someone is a terrible imprecation.

However, Cromwell settled many of his troops in Ireland and they became assimilated like so many before them.

King Billy, the Apprentice Boys, and the Battle of the Boyne

When King Charles returned to England to accept the throne in 1660 many Irishmen hoped to get their lands back. But Charles was only restored at the invitation of Parliament and could do nothing. In 1685 Charles's brother James, a Catholic, became King. James II made himself so unpopular that William of Orange, the Dutch ruler (married to James's sister Mary), was invited to take over the English throne.

James turned to Ireland, where in 1689 he attempted to stage a comeback and was welcomed by the Catholic population. They had backed the wrong horse. James was denied entry to the City of Londonderry when thirteen Protestant apprentice boys seized the keys and shut the gates in his face. Thirty thousand Protestants were besieged in the city for 105 days, while an English fleet looked on and failed to help them. To this day Protestant Loyalists still prefer to trust to themselves rather than the English.

When called to give in they replied "No Surrender," and this phrase has been the watchword of the Northern Irish Protestants ever since.

On July 12, 1690, William of Orange, riding a white horse, defeated the Catholic Irish under James at the Battle of the Boyne. King Billy and his white horse are still to be seen painted on the side of many Belfast end-of-terrace houses, together with the words "1690 No Surrender!"

James fled to Dublin, where he complained that the Irish (who actually fought very hard) had run away. A lady present remarked "Your Majesty won the race!" James II is not a popular figure in Irish history and it would be as well not to translate his nickname, *Seamus a Chaca*. It is not unconnected with what flows through sewers!

The Penal Laws

The Protestant victory led to the enactment of the "Penal Laws" against Catholics in 1695. These placed severe restrictions on landownership by Catholics, which caused many landowners to convert to the Anglican Church of Ireland. By 1778 when the penal laws began to be repealed only 5 percent of the land was Catholic owned.

The Protestant Ascendancy

The eighteenth century was the age of the "Protestant Ascendancy" when many of Ireland's great houses were built and Dublin acquired its beautiful redbrick Georgian squares. Dublin became a fashionable center, and Ireland had its own Parliament (Catholics were excluded of course). The old Parliament building is now the Bank of Ireland.

It was said that "the Church of Ireland fell asleep during the eighteenth century," but if the Anglican clergy of Ireland were not distinguished for their piety, several became famous in other ways. Jonathan Swift, author of *Gulliver's Travels* and other satirical works, was Dean of St. Patrick's Cathedral, Bishop Berkeley was a famous philosopher, and John Hervey wrote an important account of the court of George II. Nonclerical products of the Protestant Ascendancy include the chemist Robert Boyle, the politician Edward Burke, and the writers Richard Sheridan and Oliver Goldsmith.

The United Irishmen and the '98

In the late eighteenth century the American and French Revolutions inspired risings by the mainly Protestant "United Irishmen" led by Wolfe Tone and Lord Edward Fitzgerald. In 1796 a French fleet of thirty-five ships crammed with thousands of troops fresh from victories all over Europe anchored off Bantry Bay. But a week of fierce gales made it impossible for them to land and they sailed away.

The English soldiers' cruel floggings of anyone they thought might reveal information about the United Irishmen were largely responsible for the rising known as "the '98" two years later. Now no well-armed French professionals arrived to take on the British. Instead the Irish had to make do with their traditional weapons—homemade pikes manufactured by the local blacksmiths. After some minor successes the rebels were easily crushed at the battle of Vinegar Hill outside Wexford. In the North the Presbyterians, who also suffered under the Penal Laws, actively supported the rebellion, and Henry Joy McCracken led a force that captured Antrim town from the British garrison.

The failure of the '98 led to Ireland being incorporated into the United Kingdom under the Act of Union of 1801, and to the end of a separate Irish Parliament.

Robert Emmet led an abortive rising in Dublin in 1803, which proved a fiasco, but his speech from the dock when he was condemned to death has rung down the years.

"Let no man write my epitaph. When my country takes her place among the nations of the earth, then and not till then let my epitaph be written."

The Liberator
Daniel O'Connell, born into one of the few remaining families of prosperous Catholic landowners, is still known as "the Liberator." He held mass meetings—one at Tara numbered

nearly a million people—and pressured the British government into granting basic civil rights and full Catholic emancipation in 1829. Irish Catholics could now sit in Parliament at Westminster, Catholic bishops and archbishops were accepted, and many Catholic churches were built.

THE MAKING OF MODERN IRELAND

The Great Famine and Emigration

A series of events since 1845 have had a colossal significance in defining not just the political and economic structure of modern Ireland but also its culture. These key events are the Famine and Emigration, Evictions and the Land Acts, the Gaelic Revival, the Easter Rising and the "Tan War," the Treaty of 1921, and the Irish Civil War.

Although Ireland is so much farther from America than it is from Britain, separated by the "wild and wasteful" Atlantic, since the mid-nineteenth century there has been a great sense of kinship between the Americans and the Irish. When John F. Kennedy was elected President, many Irish people saw him as "their" president. Galway even renamed its main square "Kennedy Square."

The key occurrence in this orientation toward America was the Great Hunger of the 1840s. Folk memories of those terrible times are an important facet of the Irish psyche.

The population of Ireland had burgeoned in the early nineteenth century. The country people became dependent on a single crop, the potato, which was nutritious and easy to grow. But when the entire crop was destroyed by blight in the mid-1840s a million died and huge numbers of others emigrated to America.

Three years in a row the potato crop failed, and the suffering of the people became dreadful. And all the while the British government did virtually nothing about it.

There were widespread deaths from starvation and from typhus, known as "famine fever." Even those who fled to America often died in the crowded, unsanitary "coffin ships." And all the while, in accordance with the new belief in Free Trade, food was being exported in bulk to Britain. All this led to a terrible sense of betrayal.

"I ventured through the parish this day to ascertain the condition of the inhabitants and although a man not easily moved, I confess myself unmanned by the extent and density of suffering I witnessed, more especially among the women and little children, crowds of whom were seen scattered over the turnip fields, like a flock of famished crows devouring the raw turnips, and

mostly half naked, shivering in the snow and
sleet, uttering exclamations of despair, while their
children were screaming with hunger. I am a
match for anything else I may meet here, but this
I cannot stand."
Captain Wynne, Inspecting Officer, West Clare, 1846

The "Great Hunger" sowed in Irish hearts a
profound bitterness not toward the English
people but toward the English government. It is
the central defining event of Ireland's history.

By contrast huge gratitude was felt toward the
people and government of the United States for
taking in so many of its victims. Both these
feelings remain a very significant factor in Irish
life even today.

"What captivity was to the Jews, exile has been to
the Irish. America and American influence has
educated them."
Oscar Wilde, 1889

It was long years before the Irish population
got back to a fraction of what it had been in 1840.
Indeed there are still said to be more Irish living
in New York than in Dublin. After the Famine
Ireland's population fell from eight to six million,

and it was to fall much lower before it recovered to the present 5.5 million.

"The Great Hunger" explains the much-admired lack of crowding in Ireland, the spaciousness, the quiet roads. The Irish population was reduced by 20 percent. At least a million died, but the rest of the population loss was caused by the huge scale of emigration to America, Australia, New Zealand, and Canada. And to Britain, where the men, leaving behind their families and womenfolk, worked as laborers on the railways, the so-called "navvies"—short for navigators.

The Irish Have Long Memories
The Great Famine of one hundred fifty or more years ago is not forgotten. On a recent album Sinead O'Connor sings a number entitled "Famine."

Soon after the Famine a new word entered the vocabulary of Rebellion: "Fenian." Named after the *Fianna*, the legendary Finn McCool's band of heroes, the Fenians were pledged to wage guerrilla war against the British, and American-Irish emigrants held rallies to raise money for them.

The world's first submarine was invented clandestinely by John Philip Holland (1841–1914), a former member of the Catholic teaching order, the Christian Brothers. It was known as "the Fenian Ram" and was financed by the American Fenians in the hope that it would prove the answer to Britain's naval supremacy.

But the Irish cause was to make its greatest gains in this period by political, rather than by violent action.

The Home Rule Movement

In the later nineteenth century Charles Stewart Parnell, leader of the Irish Parliamentary Party in the British House of Commons, dominated Irish politics. His aim was to achieve "Home Rule," with Ireland remaining subject to Queen Victoria but governing itself. His eighty MPs were in a powerful position since they held the balance between the two main parties, the Conservatives and Liberals, but he was assisted by the fact that Gladstone, the Liberal leader, sympathized with his views.

Parnell fought savagely against absentee Irish landlords living in England who were evicting their small tenants to consolidate their Irish lands into more viable and profitable units. It was Parnell who suggested in a speech in 1880 that those responsible for carrying out the actual evictions should be ostracized. "You must show what you think of him . . . by isolating him from the rest of his kind as if he were a leper of old, you must show him your detestation of the crime he has committed."

Boycotting

In so doing Parnell introduced a new word into the English language. The first victim of this treatment was a Captain Boycott, who was a land agent in County Mayo. Ever since the word "boycott" has been used for this sort of action.

Parnell fell from office because it became known he was having an affair with a married woman, which alienated him from his Catholic following. He was deposed in December 1890 and was dead within the year.

Gladstone proposed several Home Rule bills that were defeated in the House of Lords, but he and his party had more success with laws that enabled tenants to buy their own land. The state bought out the landlords and advanced mortgages to the former tenants that worked out to be a lot less than they had been paying as rent. Further "Land Purchase Acts" in 1903 and 1909 led to the principle of compulsory sale by the landlords, so that even before Independence the Catholic former tenants already owned the greater part of the agricultural land in Ireland.

The Irish Love of the Land

The Land laws explain why Irish agriculture takes the form of thousands of small farms, rather than large tracts as in America or even Britain. Irish farmers are fiercely attached to their land, which for so many years was taken from them.

Partly because of the Land Acts, political action took something of a back seat for a while (apart from Trade Union agitation in Dublin led by Liverpool Irishman James Larkin). Instead there was the Gaelic Revival. This was a great reassertion of Celtic culture, including Gaelic sports, the Irish language, Irish music, and Irish mythology, that had an immense influence in reviving Irish self-respect and awareness of a unique national identity.

Independence and Partition

When the First World War broke out in 1914 thousands of Irishmen volunteered for the British Army. So when to everyone's surprise a rising occurred in Dublin at Easter 1916 and the insurgents seized the General Post Office, the rebels were far from popular. But the brutal execution of the leaders (two who escaped execution were a Corkman, Michael Collins, and a Spaniard with an Irish mother, Eamon de Valera) revived all the old anti-British feelings. The poet W. B. Yeats, one of the leaders of the Celtic Revival, wrote that all was:

. . . changed, changed utterly:
A terrible beauty is born

A minor political party called *Sinn Fein* (pronounced "SHIN-fain" and meaning "Ourselves Alone") became identified with the rising, and its members captured most of the Irish seats in the 1918 Parliament following the First World War.

Shortly after the end of the World War, guerrilla war broke out in Ireland. The Irish Republican Army under the legendary leadership of Michael Collins fought against the British Auxiliary Forces, ex-servicemen known as the "Black and Tans" from the color of their rather makeshift uniforms. Many acts of brutality occurred in the "Tan War" and the British Auxiliary Forces sometimes behaved more like terrorists than disciplined troops.

This struggle, together with the tremendous influence of American public opinion, led to the Anglo-Irish Treaty in 1921, whereby twenty-six of the thirty-two counties were granted the status of a "Free State," but remained subservient in various important matters. The refusal of many Irishmen to accept these limitations led to the Civil War of 1921–2.

The Origin of the Main Irish Political Parties
The party that refused to accept the treaty became known as *Fianna Fail* (pronounced "Fina-fall"). Those who were prepared to accept it ultimately

became the *Fine Gael* (pronounced "Feen-gale"). They won the war but at the cost of the assassination of Michael Collins. Fianna Fail and Fine Gael became the two main political parties in the Irish Parliament, divided not by their differing policies but by their memories.

The 1921 Treaty highlighted the problem of Northern Ireland. Before the First World War the northern Protestants led by the famous lawyer Sir Edward Carson had categorically rejected Home Rule. Rather than live in a country controlled by the Catholic majority they declared that "Ulster would fight and Ulster would be right!" and raised an army of 40,000 men armed with smuggled German rifles to show they meant business.

The Orange Order and the Twelfth of July
Every July 12 you will see men parading through the cities of Northern Ireland on the anniversary of the Battle of the Boyne. They wear orange sashes, bowler hats, and white gloves, and sometimes break into a curious shuffling dance step known as the "Orange Shuffle." They are accompanied by bands—silver bands and brass bands, but especially fife and drum bands. They are members of "the Orange Order," a society founded in 1795 and a little reminiscent of the Masons, except that it is dedicated to defending

the Protestant religion. At one time it was almost banned, but from the mid-nineteenth century it burgeoned and has taken the lead in opposing the idea of a united independent Ireland.

With the outbreak of the First World War the Ulster Volunteers patriotically enlisted in the British Army but their German rifles were hidden away in case they should be needed later. It was partly because of this threat, but more in gratitude for the "blood sacrifice" of these volunteers (who were killed almost to a man in the Battle of the Somme) that six of the nine counties of Ulster were separated from the rest of Ireland to remain part of the United Kingdom. We are still living with the results of this division more than eighty years later.

Southern Ireland, or Eire, became a republic in all but name after Fianna Fail, led by Eamon De Valera, came to power in 1932, and especially after his new constitution of 1937. Eire was actually neutral in the Second World War, but it was not until 1948 that the "Free State" declared itself a republic and left the British Commonwealth.

Throughout the early years of independence the Irish government maintained a highly protectionist economy, and Ireland had a predictably insular psychology. It remained a largely rural backwater: peaceful, charming, but with a markedly lower standard of living than its neighbors and an economy still dominated by the British market.

To add to Ireland's difficulties, De Valera refused to continue repaying the British government loans that had enabled farmers to buy their land. The result was an economic war that lasted six years and did nothing to improve the Irish economy or North/South relations, except perhaps between the thousands of smugglers on both sides of the border.

De Valera's new constitution of 1937 outlawed both contraception and divorce and implied, nicely but categorically, that a woman's place was in the home. Whereas elsewhere in Europe the number of women in work was constantly increasing, in Ireland the figure decreased. Emigration was still the easiest way for the young and energetic to improve their lot—and it is claimed that of the generation of men born between 1931 and 1941, 80 percent emigrated.

America and Australia remained the preferred destinations, but the chances of returning were small. Many young Irishmen left the countryside to earn better money in England in the building trade. They lived in dreary single rooms in the London districts of Kilburn and Cricklewood. Most of them intended to make enough money to return to Ireland and marry, but all too many never did.

All this has changed drastically in the last forty years, and to anyone who knew Eire in the 1950s the transformation could well appear little short of miraculous. Yet it continues at breakneck speed.

THE MAIN IRISH CITIES

Irish cities are usually compact, so that you are aware that they are set in the countryside. Belfast is a typical industrial conurbation but you have only to look upward to see the empty hills that surround three sides of the city. Even in Dublin, much the largest of Irish cities, you can catch glimpses of the blue hills and a short drive brings you into unspoiled country.

Dublin

Dublin is both the Irish capital and the capital of the province of Leinster. Like most of Ireland's great cities it was in practice founded by the Danes. *Dubh-linn* literally means "Blackpool," but that wasn't poetic enough for the founders of the Irish State. Its official Irish name is *Baile Atha*  *Cliath* ("BOLL-yah AW-hah CLEE-ah"), "the Town on the Ford of the Hurdles," commemorating Conor McNessa, King of Ulster, who built a bridge of hurdles across the swollen River Liffey. But everyone calls the place Dublin.

It is home to about a million today, more if you count the outlying suburbs. Dublin exports, among other things, stout and whiskey, glass and cigarettes. It also makes microprocessors and is the seat of Parliament.

Despite unforgivable municipal vandalism in the 1960s and 1970s, Dublin is still, at least in part, a town of lovely Georgian squares and of open parks and greens. Phoenix Park is the largest walled park in Europe, and herds of deer roam in it.

Naturally Dublin has the National Museum and National Art Gallery, but Ireland's greatest national treasure, the eighth-century Book of Kells, said to be the most beautiful book in the world, is to be found in Trinity College. Trinity was founded in 1591 to promote Anglicanism and is now known as Dublin University. University College, for Catholics, where James Joyce studied, became part of the, separate, National University of Ireland in 1909. There is also now a third university in the city: the Dublin City University.

There are far too many interesting sights to include here. Dublin even has two cathedrals, both Anglican—the Catholics have to make do with a "pro-Cathedral" in a back street. Serious tourists should buy one of the many good city guides that are readily available.

Cork

Cork (population 180,000) is the Republic's second city. It is reputedly the friendliest city in Ireland and its citizens the most talkative in a generally garrulous country. They were also famous rebels. The Cork Column was one of the most successful units in the war against the Black and Tans, and in retaliation in 1920 Cork was deliberately set on fire by them and its Sinn Fein Lord Mayor killed. His successor, Terence MacSwiney, died in jail in London after a hunger strike.

Cork City is on the River Lee; its streets are built over waterways where ships would have been anchored. Like Dublin it was founded by the Vikings—or Danes as they are called in Ireland. But before that St. Finbar had established a monastery there. St. Finn Barre's Anglican Cathedral is a splendid Gothic Revival building built between 1865 and 1880.

The port, called Cobh, mainly exports agricultural produce. Cork is well known for its gin, its whiskey, for Beamish stout, and for Father Matthew. When Cork people talk of "the Statue," they mean that of Father Theobald Matthew (his name is spelled "Mathew" on its plinth). Father Matthew founded the Catholic temperance movement that became the Pioneers. The success of the Pioneers is one of several reasons why the image of the drunken Irish is not borne out by the actual statistics of alcohol consumption.

Blarney Castle is in the vicinity, where thousands of tourists lean backward and nearly break their necks in order to kiss an unhygienic bit of rock called the blarney stone in the belief that it will give them the gift of the gab.

Galway

Galway, way out in the west, is the capital of bleakly beautiful Connaught. It is a wonderfully lively city with huge numbers of young people, mainly students, who make up 20 percent of its 60,000 population. It is full of musical pubs, is a center for the Gaelic language, and is the gateway to the Aran Islands.

Limerick

Limerick, on the Shannon estuary, has a population of just under 60,000. Occupied by the Vikings in the ninth century it became the capital of the province, then Kingdom, of Munster at about the time the Irish king Brian Boru defeated the Vikings at the battle of Clontarf in 1014.

Belfast

Belfast's population is about 300,000, but half a million people live within ten miles of the city, accounting for about a third of the entire population of the province of Northern Ireland. Queen's University was founded in 1845, and the Northern Irish Assembly is at Stormont, a Belfast suburb.

The city was founded in 1177 but remained tiny until the textile industry was stimulated by the arrival of French Protestants (Huguenots), fleeing persecution in the late seventeenth century. Its location on the deep waters of Belfast Lough made it a great center for shipbuilding—the *Titanic* was built at Harland and Woolff's yard there. This and the linen boom of the nineteenth century meant the population swelled from 20,000 in 1800 to 387,000 in 1911.

The city center has been redeveloped over the last twenty years, and today Belfast has an air of real vitality, helped by the fact the last thirty years have seen a major literary renaissance in Northern Ireland.

By 1939 Belfast had more people than Dublin. But the traditional industries were already in decline, and terrible air raids during the war, together with the effects of the troubles from 1969 onward, led to a drop in population and high unemployment, which peaked in the 1980s. Quieter times since the cease-fire and the power-sharing agreements of the 1990s seem to be leading to a significant recovery.

Londonderry

Londonderry, or Derry to its mainly Catholic population, is the province's only other major city. Its most important industry is shirtmaking, which started in the 1820s. Set on the Foyle estuary in the west of the province it has a population of about 65,000. St. Columba founded the first monastery here in the sixth century when it was called Derry. It became Londonderry during the plantation of Ulster, when it was handed over to the Corporation of the City of London to be "planted" with English Protestant settlers, though even today two-thirds of its inhabitants are Catholic.

In 1689 the city held out for 105 days against James II's forces before being relieved. The Catholic Bogside area was frequently in the news during the troubles between 1968 and the 1990s.

POLITICS IN THE REPUBLIC

Eire is a parliamentary democracy with a written constitution and a two-chamber parliament, the *Oireachtas* (pronounced "ERR-ockh-tuss"). The senate, *Seanad Eireann* ("SHAN-ud-AIR-un") has a total of sixty members, forty-nine elected by the Universities and by five vocational panels, and eleven nominated by the Prime Minister, the *Taoiseach* ("TEE-shock"). The important chamber is the house of representatives, the *Dail Eireann*, ("DAW-il AIR-un"), whose 166 members are elected by a complex form of proportional representation.

Elections are every five years. Fundamental changes (divorce being a recent example) have to be approved by referendum. The President, who is directly elected every seven years, does not exercise an executive role. However, supreme command of the defense forces is vested in the President who also receives and credits ambassadors and carries out ceremonial duties. Real power lies with the *Taoiseach* (formally appointed by the President), who sits in the *Dail* as an elected member.

Friends in the Police

The Irish police force, the *Garda Siachana* ("Garda shickhana"), usually called "the Garda," is unarmed. The Garda are well integrated into the community, and visitors should not hesitate to call on their services.

Criticizing politicians is a popular Irish pastime, but the complexity of the Irish political system with its many nuances is likely to discourage outsiders from joining in.

Up to the 1980s, the civil war that followed independence in 1921 formed a basic dividing line in the Irish political system. The oldest political party in Ireland is the Labor Party, dating back to the time of James Larkin, the Trade Union leader, but the two dominant parties were Fianna Fail and Fine Gael.

However, at last the hatreds of the civil war seem to have faded away and, aided by a voting system that works against overall majorities for any one party, coalitions seem to have replaced single-party government. In the 1992 cabinet, for instance, the *Tanaiste* ("TARN-ash-ta") or Deputy Prime Minister was the leader of the Labor Party.

New parties have also emerged. The Progressive Democrats are a splinter group from Fianna Fail, and the Democratic Left, which was the party supporting the IRA, has now become a soft-left party. Its old role has been taken over by the reemergence of the Sinn Fein (which also contests elections in Northern Ireland) which made an impressive showing in the 2002 elections to the *Dail*.

The election in 1990 of a liberal woman, Mary Robinson, as President was seen by many as marking a shift in Irish politics away from conservative stereotypes. It was such a success that another woman, Mary McAleese, succeeded her.

Significantly articles 2 and 3 of the Irish Constitution, which lay claim to Northern Ireland as part of a United Ireland, have now been amended to require this change only with the consent of the people of the North.

NORTHERN IRELAND TODAY

The problem of Northern Ireland remains to plague the island and there has been much blood spilled since it flared up again in 1969. The issues are immensely complicated yet also simple. Two-thirds of the people are of Scots or English stock, Plantation Protestants who have no desire to break with Britain and join the Catholic Irish of the Republic. The rest are native Irish Catholics, most of whom would prefer to be part of a united independent Ireland.

And just to muddle things even more, everybody in Ireland, North and South, is entitled to an Irish passport, and all Irish citizens have full rights of citizenship in the United Kingdom!

But things in the North are looking up and, while some violence still occurs, Northern Ireland has genuinely been transformed by the cease-fire of October 1994, which was underlined and given a special dimension by President Clinton's visit in 1995.

The two most encouraging events since 1995 have been the Good Friday Agreement of 1998, and the consequent establishment of the power-sharing Northern Irish Assembly at Stormont.

WHAT IS THE GOOD FRIDAY AGREEMENT?
The Good Friday Agreement of 1998 provided a three-stranded solution. There is an elected Assembly and Executive, representative of both political traditions in Northern Ireland, and there are cross-border bodies to develop cooperation between both parts of the island. An East-West dimension is designed to improve relationships between Ireland and mainland Britain.

POLITICS IN NORTHERN IRELAND

There are twelve political parties, of which five matter. The moderate parties are the Social Democratic and Labor Party and the Alliance Party, who try to bring Catholics and Protestants together. The SDLP was founded in 1970 by Gerry Fitt, a Catholic Union leader, and John Hume, a teacher. In 1996 "Saint John" won the Nobel Peace Prize and donated the money to the poor and to victims of violence in the North.

The Loyalists are chiefly represented by the Unionist Party, which was the ruling party from

Partition until the original Stormont Parliament was abolished in 1972. David Trimble, its leader, is the Chief Executive of the Northern Irish Assembly, and is committed to power-sharing in the new Assembly.

Sinn Fein was the political wing of the IRA, but has now emerged in its own right as the main party of the Catholic Republicans, gaining ground from the SDLP. Its charismatic leaders are Gerry Adams and Martin McGuinness. McGuinness is the Minister of Education in the new Assembly. Both have been elected to the House of Commons at Westminster but cannot take their seats because they refuse to take the oath to the Queen.

The Good Friday Agreement was the direct result of discussions between Adams and Hume, who were later joined by David Trimble.

The Democratic Unionists, Ian Paisley's party, has maintained a hard-core form of Unionism opposed to any concessions to the Republicans and still has considerable support.

The New Assembly
The Assembly has 108 seats elected by a form of proportional representation, a vastly fairer elective system than the old system of "gerrymandering" that guaranteed Protestant majorities in local government. Ministerial seats are allocated in direct proportion to the strengths

of the various parties. If it is to work, both sides will have to tear up a lot of history books.

Death Rate in Northern Ireland

Although the Troubles in Northern Ireland have taken up so many newspaper headlines over the years, even during the worst times life went on as usual. Throughout the period no tourist was ever killed and Northern Ireland had the lowest death rate in the whole of the United Kingdom!

Northern Ireland has much to offer the visitor or businessperson. The EU has already done a lot to break down the economic barriers between the two countries, and free trade may help dissolve other barriers as well. Whatever visitors do or say to empathize positively in the desire for a lasting peace will be warmly welcomed.

chapter two

VALUES & ATTITUDES

IRISHNESS

Every Englishman seems to have a fixed idea of the Irish—from Shakespeare in *Henry V* to the man next to you in the London pub asking you if you have heard the joke about the two Irishmen. However what one Englishman wrote about the Irish four hundred years ago does perhaps have a grain of truth in it. Richard Stanyhurst's "Description of Ireland" forms part of Holinshed's Chronicles, published in 1578.

> *"The people are thus inclined: religious, frank, amorous, ireful, sufferable of infinite pains, very vainglorious, many sorcerers, excellent horsemen, delighted with wars, great almsgivers, surpassing in hospitality. The lewder sort are sensual and loose in living. The same being virtuously bred up or reformed, are such mirrors of holiness and austerity that other nations retain but a shadow in comparison of them . . . Greedy of praise they be and fearful of dishonour."*

Certainly the Irish are religious, love horses, and reckon they are more capable of hard physical labor than anyone else. The Irish country people are wonderfully hospitable, and the Irish as a whole give more to charity per head than any nation in Europe. To say they delight in wars may be an exaggeration, but famous soldiers of Irish descent in the two world wars include Lord Kitchener, Field Marshal Montgomery, Earl Alexander of Tunis, Field Marshal Alanbrooke, and Lawrence of Arabia (not to mention Peter O'Toole who played him in the film of the same name). The first winner of the Victoria Cross, the highest British military award, was an Irishman, Charles David Lucas.

If the Irish do not seem austere, remember they are capable of going on hunger strike and "suffering infinite pains" to the extent of starving themselves to death for a cause they believe in.

They are often holy, and Ireland is a land of saints, but also one of scholars, writers, poets, and playwrights. The Irish are proud of their ancient and rich culture: poetry, drama, music, singing, and dance are not something special to be separated off as "the Arts," but part of everyday life shared by the whole community. They are the means by which they express their own identity.

Then there is Irish folklore, with its heroes, larger than life characters such as Finn McCool; its heroines, like Deirdre of the Sorrows; and the stories of the Leprechauns and other fairies. People may or may not believe in them, but they are important as part of the national consciousness.

Are the Irish vainglorious? They speak proudly of their status as "a nation once again" and of the centuries-long struggle that won that freedom. You will find the ordinary people of Ireland much more aware of their nation's history than are most Europeans.

As to whether the Irish are "ireful," there is maybe a glimmer of truth in the words Shakespeare gives to Captain Macmorris in *Henry V*: "I do not know you so good a man as myself, so Chrish save me, I will cut off your head."

Greedy of Praise?

Oliver St. John Gogarty, one of the great Irish wits (he appears in Joyce's *Ulysses* as Buck Mulligan), once wrote that "You should never praise one Irishman to another." And there is perhaps a tendency for Irishmen to criticize each other. When I asked a prosperous Irish businessman I know if he could give me any tips for the chapter on doing business in Ireland his only response was "The Irish! I wouldn't do business with those b—ds!"

Their religion matters to the Irish. Again history provides the key. For years the penal laws proscribed Catholicism, yet 90 percent of those in the southern counties of Ireland remained true to the old faith. More people attend church in Ireland than anywhere else in Europe. And not just Catholics: the Protestants of the North also see their faith as a central reality in their lives and in their identity as a community.

Everyone in Ireland speaks English, but 100,000 or so also speak the ancient Irish language and everyone learns it in school. And if some have resented the long hours spent studying its complex grammar, they would still hate to see it disappear. They like to use a few familiar phrases in everyday conversation—even if it is only to wish you *slainte* ("SLARN-cha"), good health! On the other hand, you may sometimes see someone with a little gold badge in their lapel; this is the *fainne* ("FARN-nya"), a symbol that they are a fluent Irish speaker.

The Irish are a passionate people and this sometimes makes them narrow-minded or even bigoted in their opinions. Politics within the Republic of Ireland no longer excites people as much as it did in the decades following the brief but bitter civil war, but of course the overwhelming Irish political issue is still Northern Ireland.

Don't Get Involved!

Our advice is not to get involved in arguments about the politics of Northern Ireland, but equally not to be worried about visiting the North. Nowadays life is much more settled and there is a great desire for peace on all sides; you will find a beautiful countryside, a progressive economy, and a people as friendly, obliging, and welcoming as everywhere else in Ireland.

Of course it might take an effort to avoid becoming involved in a political discussion—the Irish do love a good argument. But then they love any kind of talk, being a convivial people, and are genuinely interested in you and what you have to say.

Even if you have come to Ireland on business people will want to find out about you and your family. You can actually cause offense if you try to cut through these courtesies and get down to the work at hand too quickly. Like the man in the pub who suggests you should "hold your hour and have another," the Irish are no great respecters of the tyranny of the clock—if the talk is good why not let it flow for a while? And before you condemn them for this, don't forget they have one of the most flourishing economies in Europe.

THE IRISH VIEW OF THE OUTSIDE WORLD

Parallel with Ireland's huge economic changes has been a remarkable change in the Irish view of the outside world. The decades after independence were marked by a sense of introversion, a desire to concentrate on domestic matters. Those who did not like this attitude were free to leave—and they did, in their millions. However the abandonment of protectionism in the 1960s was also the beginning of a new approach to the outside world.

The young people of Ireland now see the world as their oyster, and new graduates may spend several years abroad before returning to take jobs at home. Naturally many go to New York or Sydney, but there are substantial pockets of Irish in places as diverse as continental Europe and Japan.

The Irish have learned they have nothing to fear from the outside world, indeed that their lives can be enriched by positively embracing it. The international repute of Irish literature helps: the world is now a stage on which the Irish can find a global audience for their national culture. Irish prosperity means that those staying at home have to cope with large numbers of foreigners in their midst, and dealing with significant immigration is proving a challenge for a country where emigration was the fate of so many for so long.

IRELAND TODAY

From the early 1930s onward Ireland's prime ministers were drawn from the leaders of the struggle for independence, men like Eamon de Valera and the former IRA officer Sean McBride, traditionalists concerned with preserving the values they had fought for. But in 1959 the aging de Valera was replaced by Sean Lamass, who was determined to open up the country's economy and cut back the loss of so many young people to England, Australia, and America.

By the mid-1960s emigration had halved and many who had left had chosen to return to a country that now seemed much more progressive and full of opportunity. (Today immigration runs at an annual figure of about 50,000.) Ireland had become more outward looking, and it was not merely looking westward to the United States.

The European Union

In 1972 both the Republic and Northern Ireland (as part of the United Kingdom) joined the European Union, and this became a factor of enormous importance in the transformation of the country.

The EU has benefited the country economically by investment in industry, by paying for the rapidly improving road network, by modernizing the fishing fleet, and in a thousand other ways. It has made it possible for the Republic to diversify away from its claustrophobic one-on-one relationship with Britain and to emerge as a modern European power, increasingly confident in her own distinctive identity. Today the United Kingdom only accounts for about a third of Irish exports and less than half of Irish imports. On the other hand, the Irish are losing control of their own economic destiny, with foreign-owned companies responsible for half the total turnover and employing almost half the workforce.

After the initial boost of joining the EU, Ireland did, in fact, suffer an economic setback in the early 1980s, and emigration increased again. But a further recovery began in the 1990s and, at the time of writing, the Irish economy is performing exceptionally well and seems likely to continue doing so. Tourism, in particular, is enjoying a boom throughout the island, which is marketed as a single entity, North and South, by the tourist industry worldwide.

SEX AND MORALITY
The influence of the EU is all-pervasive and its impact goes beyond material improvements. European legislation has also effected changes in areas such as sexual equality. However the Catholic

Church remains a powerful conservative moral force in the Republic, and divorce was still illegal until it was narrowly accepted by a referendum in 1995—Ireland was the last nation in Europe to legalize it. Contraception, too, is still a controversial issue.

> *"The Catholic Church already possesses an efficient contraceptive. It consists in the word, 'No!'"*
>
> **Irish Bishop speaking in the early 1970s**

Abortion is no longer officially illegal in the Republic, but is not carried out there. The Irish abortion rate is believed to approach the Western average, but Irish women go abroad for it.

Homosexuality is also now legal, though only since 1993. It is a measure of how quickly attitudes toward sexual mores are being revolutionized that David Norris, who is openly gay, is both the Senator for Trinity College and a frequent guest on television chat shows.

However, perhaps it is not fair to attribute the Republic's conservatism in sexual matters wholly to the influence of the Catholic Church. Long after legislation was introduced in England, Protestant Northern Ireland continued to prosecute both homosexuality and abortion in law.

A recent survey found that 18 percent of all children in the Republic are now born outside marriage (the figure for Northern Ireland is 20 percent), and most young people are not especially worried about chastity before marriage. On the other hand, promiscuity is rare and partners tend to stay together. Within marriage, too, the survey found, sexual faithfulness remains strong.

CENSORSHIP AND BAD LANGUAGE

Moral censorship used to be a significant aspect of life in the Republic, both through the Censorship Board and at the local level where even the books on the library shelves could come under ban. Ridicule proved a potent enemy, and the huge list of banned books has been vastly reduced. Something of a breakthrough occurred when the film *Priest* about sex and scandal in the Catholic Church was actually shown publicly in Dublin.

Though scandals about money matters occur in Irish politics at both local and national levels, the sort of sexual shenanigans that so enliven British politics are not generally featured in Irish political life. Clerical scandals are quite another matter. There have been many sexual scandals within the Catholic Church. Recently, when an elderly priest died in a gay sauna, two younger priests were on hand to give him the last rites!

Mind Your Language!

The Irish love talk but are no lovers of bad language. The casual use of obscenities in conversation that might not raise an eyebrow in England can cause embarrassment and offense. They have a rather charming habit of defusing obscene words by changing one letter—hence the often heard adjective "fecking." James Joyce's *Ulysses*, which was banned in both England and Ireland when it was published in 1922, is famously sexually explicit. But Joyce knew his countrymen well and the only characters who actually utter the "F-word" or any other obscenities are a pair of drunken English soldiers.

In 1990 Ireland elected its first woman president, and though the powers of the President hardly compare to those of the Prime Minister, Mary Robinson did much to alter the government's traditional social attitudes and bring them more in line with those of many young people. It is worth noting that Ireland now has more women MPs than there are in the much larger British Parliament.

SOCIAL ATTITUDES AND THE TV SCREEN

A now-dead member of the *Oireachtas* (Parliament) once famously claimed there had been no sex in Ireland before television. In a sense he was right: the developing openness about sexuality in Ireland is a by-product of television breaking down old taboos.

Television has been a key factor in changing social attitudes. Irish television's *Late Late Show* provided a forum for debating the essential issues of Irish life for more than a generation, but of even greater significance has been the widespread availability of British Television through satellite and cable. A high proportion of all households in Dublin have been cabled for more than twenty years, and now most of the country is covered. British Television has helped form the consciousness of the under-forty generation— now a majority in the population—and has profoundly influenced the evolution of society.

chapter three

RELIGION & TRADITION

RELIGION IS IMPORTANT

Catholic Ireland is an obviously religious country; there are shrines by the roadside, huge parking lots around the churches accommodate the crowds coming to Mass on Sundays, and drivers in the Republic will cross themselves whenever they pass a church or a shrine. The Northern Protestants are scarcely less devout; their churches attract congregations that rival those of the Catholics. More than 50 percent of people in Northern Ireland are churchgoers compared to 15 percent in the rest of the U.K.

The Presbyterian Church in Northern Ireland and the Roman Catholic Church in Eire are so much part of the ethos of each of these two communities that, for better or worse, the separate identities of the Nationalist Republic and the Loyalist Province seem to be bound in with where their citizens pray on Sundays.

Visitors must understand that religion is a hugely significant element in Irish cultural, domestic, and political life, even though the traditional all-pervasive influence of the Roman Catholic Church in southern Irish communities is becoming increasingly a thing of the past.

THE CATHOLIC CHURCH IN IRELAND

This old unquestioning faith in the Catholic Church's moral authority, which was much strengthened with the coming of Irish independence, has been undermined by scandals about pedophile priests and a well-known and well-liked bishop who was found to be supporting a mistress and a son out of Church funds. In any case Irish men and women are today less willing to accept unquestioningly the Church's teaching on such matters as contraception, and young people, as elsewhere in Western Europe, are increasingly seeing belief as a personal matter and open acknowledgment of Church membership as almost embarrassing.

"Believing is a lonely business in my generation. It's a bit like the Irish language. Unless you go to a special club you don't expect to find others who speak it fluently. Or perhaps being religious is like being gay: it's not something you admit to everyone straight off. Faith has certainly gone shy."
Young Irishman in conversation with Jesuit priest

Nevertheless southern Ireland still has the highest percentage of regular churchgoers in Western Europe. Go to any village and you will see most of the community at Mass on Sunday.

"On Sunday mornings in Ireland, no-one seeing the great crowds making their way to and from Mass could have any doubt about Ireland's devotion to the Mass."
Pope John Paul II speaking in Dublin 1979

Recent figures suggest that 60 percent of all Irish attend Mass weekly. Throughout Ireland, North and South, the Roman Catholic Church claims a membership of 3,989,5601, accounting for some 75 percent of the population

Of this number, some 3,000 are priests active in the parish. And active means active! No longer is the word of the priest law, but what he has to say still matters. This is partly because he is likely to be involved in all aspects of the life of his parish, including joining in the plays at the drama group or running the local dance—activities his predecessors would have castigated.

But it is indicative of changing attitudes that there are fewer recruits to keep up the numbers. In 1997 for instance there were only fifty-three ordinations. In a country where half the population is under thirty, half the priests are over fifty.

As in other Catholic countries the Irish enjoy their religious festivals, and colorful quasi-public ceremonies are held to mark the major festivals such as Easter, Pentecost, and the feast of Corpus Christi (on July 17). Visitors will see children dressed in full regalia for their "First Communion." The young girls dressed as miniature brides seem particularly strange to those unfamiliar with the ritual.

Enjoy St. Patrick's Day: No Kissing Please!
St. Patrick's Day (March 17) is still a religious holiday in Ireland. While some of the razzmatazz that surrounds it in America has been exported back to Ireland in recent years, do not expect green beer or the "kiss me, I'm Irish!" exuberance of the American experience. A get-together with friends or clubbing is more likely.

EDUCATION: EIRE
Many aspects of Irish life continue to be organized on denominational lines, especially education. Until very recently the Catholic Church was the leading provider of education in Ireland, with more than 3,500 primary schools and over 800 secondary schools, North and South, which educate something like 650,000 pupils. The Anglican

Church of Ireland is also heavily involved in education in the Republic, and has its own schools.

The period of compulsory education in the Republic is from ages six to fifteen, though many students go on to take higher exams at seventeen. At fifteen students take public exams called the "Junior Certificate," and at seventeen they take the "Leaving Certificate." Since primary schools, called "National Schools," are all denominational, Protestant schoolchildren have the right to be bussed to Protestant schools. The situation does not really arise for Catholics.

After primary education, the second-level sector comprises secondary, vocational, community, and comprehensive schools, all publicly aided. Of these some 60 percent are the more academic secondary schools, which are mostly managed by the religious orders. Although the majority are Catholic, many Protestant students attend them because of the comparative lack of provision for Protestants at this level. All students have to study Gaelic, but examinations are no longer compulsory. The State meets about 95 percent of the cost of teachers' salaries.

There are four universities: Dublin (Trinity College), the University of Ireland (NUI), which embraces University College Cork (UCC), the University of Limerick, and Dublin City University.

THE IRISH WAY OF DEATH

Irish attitudes toward death are quite different from those of the English. Mourning in Ireland is public and there is no shame in showing your feelings. You would be expected to commiserate with a friend or acquaintance, in the business world or elsewhere, who has suffered a recent loss.

Funerals are an important part of everyday life. They are semipublic occasions: food and drink are provided and everyone drinks to the memory of the departed. In the past, the custom known as "waking the dead" was for the body to remain in the house, and hours were spent sitting round the coffin, drinking, talking, and reminiscing. James Joyce took the title of his most notoriously difficult novel, *Finnegans Wake*, from a popular comic song about just such a wake.

You will sometimes hear the expression "an American wake." In the old days when people emigrated to America there seemed little chance that they would ever see their friends and relatives again. They were passing out of their lives as if they were dying. So a wake was held for them.

And if the Irish derive such enjoyment from a time of grief, just imagine the fun of an Irish wedding!

Irish churches do not recognize the border between Northern Ireland and the Republic, and both Catholic and Anglican bishoprics have dioceses that straddle the border.

What to Wear

Visitors will be warmly welcomed in any place of worship. It is no longer necessary to dress in one's "Sunday best" and informality is now the general rule. If in doubt, a jacket and tie for males and the equivalent for females would ensure that you are not out of place.

THE CHURCH OF IRELAND

The Anglican "Church of Ireland" is a curious anomaly. When Henry VIII broke with Rome, the Irish Parliament passed a series of acts that ended the authority of the Pope over the Church in Ireland. Most of the bishops acquiesced, since the Celtic Irish Church had only surrendered its autonomy to Rome in the twelfth century. Then in Elizabeth's reign the first English Protestant prayer book was published, and in 1550 Ireland got its first printing press to print it, and the troubles began.

Most of the Irish at that time spoke Gaelic, not English, and the book did not catch on. So the Church split between those who stayed with the Latin mass and were increasingly papist in sympathy and those, mostly the ruling classes, who adopted the Anglican rite.

In brief, the Catholics got the vast bulk of the people, but the Anglicans got the churches and cathedrals, so the tradition of outdoor Masses for

Catholics began. The weakness of the English administration in Ireland meant both Churches carried on in parallel, but the ravages of the civil wars left them both in a chaotic state.

After the defeat of the Irish forces supporting the Catholic King James II in 1690, the Church of Ireland became the only Church officially tolerated, and penal laws were brought in that attacked not only Catholicism but the Presbyterians of the North. Catholic bishops and archbishops were not officially allowed until Catholic emancipation in 1829. That is why there are two sets of bishops and archbishops across Ireland, the Roman Catholic and the Anglican.

The Church of Ireland has just over 360,000 members and about 500 clergy. Like the Catholics it is having difficulty in recruiting clergy, and only seventeen were ordained in 1998. In the Republic, rather more than in the fiercely nonconformist North, members of the Anglican community exercise an influence out of all proportion to their numbers. Many of Ireland's greatest writers came from this group.

ECUMENISM
Relations between the two denominations have been cordial since Independence in 1921. Both work hard to break down old prejudices and

antagonisms—but sometimes the mischievous Irish sense of humor cannot be suppressed even among all this mutual goodwill.

Danny Boy

Brendan Behan used to tell how the Bishop of Cork, the Most Reverend Doctor Daniel Cohalan—known affectionately to all Cork people as "Danny Boy"—lay in his last illness. He was old—he must have been about ninety-four when he died—and his illness dragged on and on. It happened that the Protestant Bishop of Cork, a very much younger man, upped and died before him. The Monsignor brought the news to "Danny Boy" and stood around waiting for the words of spiritual consolation that he would convey to the Protestant chapter. There was a long silence. After two or three minutes, "Danny Boy" opened an eye, looked at the Monsignor and said to him: "Well, he knows now who's the real Bishop of Cork!"

Despite "Danny Boy," the two Irish primates, the Catholic and Church of Ireland Archbishops of Armagh get on well—though they remain strongly divided on the issue of women in the priesthood. They regularly appear together on television to display solidity in the face of sectarian violence.

THE PRESBYTERIAN CHURCH

The North has many nonconformist sects but the dominant influence is the Presbyterian Church. In Ireland it dates back to the seventeenth-century "plantation" of Ulster by Scottish settlers. Like the Church of Scotland it has no bishops; instead elected church members run each individual congregation. The congregations are grouped into districts called Presbyteries. Ministers and elders represent their congregations at Presbytery and at regional Synods. Overall control is in the hands of the annual General Assembly, representing all the 560 congregations in Ireland. Its chief representative is the Moderator, who only serves for a single year. The ministry has been open to women since 1972.

The Presbyterian Church has 350,000 members, predominantly in the North, and 427 ministers of whom nineteen are women (figures for 1999).

EDUCATION: NORTHERN IRELAND

In Northern Ireland the basic system is the same as in the rest of the U.K., with compulsory education from five to sixteen. There are GCSE (General Certificate of Secondary Education) examinations at sixteen, with Advanced Levels at eighteen for those who want to stay on, as many do. But in contrast to elsewhere in the U.K., schooling is largely in the hands of the religious denominations, with Protestant schools predominating. There are some integrated schools, but only 14,000 pupils, or about 4 percent of the school population, attend them. Until 1992 no schools were allowed to teach the Irish language, but it is now taught at some independent schools.

There are two universities, the Queen's University of Belfast, and the University of Ulster, and many Northern Irish students go to these in preference to universities in mainland Britain. Often their time at university will be their first experience of mixing with members of a different religious community.

METHODISTS AND OTHERS

The Irish Methodist Church has 234 churches, North and South, and 60,000 members, though it serves a community double that size. Methodists have been actively involved in the peace process in the North.

There are also a number of other dissenting churches, mostly in Northern Ireland: the Baptists have 20,000 members; the Congregationalists 8,000; the Unitarians 3,000; and 90,000 people belong to a wide variety of other sects.

There are comparatively few Jews or Muslims in Ireland, even though the "hero" of Ireland's most famous or notorious work of fiction, James Joyce's *Ulysses*, was a Jew. Nevertheless the *Dail* of 1992–7 had two Jewish members and one Muslim.

But if there are only about a thousand Muslims and a thousand Jews, there are twelve and a half thousand monks and nuns.

THE RELIGIOUS ORDERS

The religious orders have a very special place in the Irish psyche. This is partly because so many people were educated by nuns, by the Christian Brothers or the Jesuits or the monks and friars of any number of other religious orders.

Seamus Heaney once described the nuns of one particularly fashionable convent as "The Little Sisters of the Rich." But though there were and are a few such convents, there are many more "Little Sisters of the Poor" working with the disadvantaged of Ireland, or in Africa and Asia, with the missionary orders of monks in schools and hospitals, and receiving generous support from the collecting boxes placed in every pub.

Another reason for the religious orders' special status is the role they have played in Irish history from the epoch of the "Island of Saints and Scholars" to the time of the penal laws, when they were proscribed and had to be hidden by the populace.

But the monks, friars, and nuns are getting older. Between 1979 and 1986 the numbers of monks and nuns dropped by a quarter and are still declining rapidly.

IRISH SAINTS

Ireland is full of local saints, historical personages from the early centuries of Irish Christianity, miracle-workers who are said to have used their sacred power to banish monsters, cure illnesses, and provide food for the people in time of need. The best-known saints have a universal appeal and are part of the national consciousness.

St. Patrick

St. Patrick, the Patron Saint and Apostle of Ireland, is associated with the conversion of the country to the Celtic, as opposed to the Roman, form of Christianity in the fifth century. The son of a Romano-British official, he was carried off into slavery by Irish raiders as a child, and for some years tended sheep in Ulster. He escaped, trained for the priesthood, probably in France, and as a result of a dream, decided to return to Ireland. Tradition says that he arrived in 432 CE, at the age of forty-seven.

He landed in the north at Strangford Lough, and hastened off to the seat of the High King at Tara. There he won the royal family over by performing miracles that were vastly more impressive than the magic of the local druids. He was also no mean arguer—he is said to have picked an argument with an angel and won!

Traditionally the shamrock became the symbol of Ireland when St. Patrick used it to illustrate the "three in one" nature of the Holy Trinity to the King of Munster.

By the time he died, probably in 475, between his arguments and his miracles Patrick had ensured that most of Ireland was officially Christian. His last years were spent in Armagh, where he died—which is why Armagh is the seat of the Catholic and Protestant primates. As to where he is buried, the Book of Armagh simply states "Where his bones rest nobody knows."

St. Brigid
St. Brigid is the most popular saint in Ireland after Patrick. As protectress of farming and livestock she has many of the attributes of the ancient earth goddess. Her feast day is significantly February 1, the Celtic pagan festival of Imbolc. It has rightly been said that she symbolizes the way Christianity did not replace the old Celtic tradition in Ireland but rather was superimposed on it.

Be that as it may, Brigid is reputed to have been born in County Kildare in 457, where she became a nun and performed many miracles. There is a charming story that when a gold cross was stolen from her convent she plaited rushes to make a cross that would be equally holy but otherwise worthless. On the eve of her festival people still plait rushes to make crosses in her name, and the Brigid's cross became one of the symbols for Irish Television—which is not to suggest that Irish Television is very holy but otherwise worthless.

St. Brendan

St. Brendan the Navigator belongs to the mid-sixth century, and was from Tralee in the south. Among the monasteries he founded was Ardfert near Tralee. It might have been even nearer to Tralee had not the plans for the foundation been seized by a crow, which flew off with them. Brendan gave  chase and where the crow dropped the plans there he built his monastery. He is most famous for the *Navigio Sancti Brendani*, which describes how he and his monks sailed to Iceland, Greenland, and possibly mainland America. In the 1970s Tim

Severin demonstrated that the ancient Irish *currachs* of wood and leather were extremely seaworthy and could have sailed across the Atlantic. Other incidents in the book seem less likely—as when Brendan met Judas Iscariot having a brief holiday from Hell clinging to a rock, or when he celebrated his Easter Mass on the back of a whale.

St. Columba

St. Columba, usually known as *Colmcille* ("Colom-keel," Colum of the Church), was a great founder of monasteries, notably Durrow (est. 548), famous for its illuminated manuscripts. He caused a battle at Cul Dreimhne in 561 in which three thousand died, and in penance went off to Scotland where he founded another famous monastery on Iona and warded off the Loch Ness monster with the sign of the Cross.

PILGRIMAGE SITES

Holy wells, dedicated to individual saints, are still frequented on their feast days in many areas; people pray at them for relief from physical and mental distress. In Synge's play *The Well of the Saints* a couple are cured of blindness at a holy well, and are distressed to find they are ugly and not beautiful as they imagined they were.

Other holy places are associated with St. Patrick: he is said to have banished snakes from Ireland standing on the summit of Croagh Patrick in Mayo. Each year thousands of pilgrims, quite a few barefoot, climb up its 2,510 feet (765 meters). In summer pilgrims go to Lough Derg (the Red Lake), where St. Patrick had a vision of Purgatory. For three days they follow the Stations of the Cross and eat one small meal a day.

At Knock, again in Mayo, in 1879 there were reports of the appearance of the Holy Family. But the bigger miracle is how a local parish priest got an enormous church (holding 20,000 people) built there and then persuaded the authorities to build an international airport!

THE IRISH LANGUAGE

By the mid-nineteenth century English was already the dominant language in much of Ireland. The

same had not been true a hundred fifty years before. Even the Londonderry apprentice boys who yelled their defiance at James II and his Catholic army would have done so in Irish.

Reward for Effort

Foreigners are not expected to understand any Irish, but the visitor who does make even a minimal effort in this direction (for instance by being aware that the Prime Minister is known by his title of *Taoiseach* (pronounced "tee-shack") will gain disproportionately in goodwill.

The Gaelic language, generally called Irish, is the oldest of the group of Celtic languages that includes Scots Gallic, Welsh, and Breton, and like them has characteristics that seem strange to English speakers. For instance Gaelic is inflected at the start of words, not the end. So, for example, the word *bad* ("bard") means boat: "his boat" is *a bad*, but "her boat" sounds completely different— *a bhad* ("vard")—and "their boat" is *a mbad* ("mard"), different again!

Before the Romans' conquest of Gaul and Britain, Celtic was the language of much of central and western Europe. Anglo-Saxon replaced it in England in the fifth century, and in Irish the English are still known as Saxons.

"*Three things no man can trust: the hoof of a horse, the horn of a bull, and the smile of a Saxon.*"
Translation of Gaelic proverb

Irish is the earliest European language north of the Alps in which extensive writings exist (see "Mythology" below). The Gaelic alphabet was developed from the Latin script in the sixth century. Prior to this the young bards were rigorously trained to commit thousands of lines to memory. To a very limited extent this verbal tradition continues to this day with a few remaining *Seanchais* ("SHAN-ak-hees"), or village storytellers, in places like the Aran Islands.

The British authorities actively suppressed the use of Irish, and for many people education went on in illegal "hedge schools" scattered through the countryside. In his play *Translations*, set in the early nineteenth century, Brian Friel portrays one such school. He also shows how when the first Ordnance Survey team arrived in Ireland to map the land, it used local people to explain the Irish names, which were then anglicized into the forms used today.

Only at the end of the century, in 1893, was the Gaelic League (*Conradh na Gaelige*, "CONRA-na-GAYLIGA") founded to revive Irish speaking. By then more than 85 percent of the population spoke only English. Today Gaelic is the first language of a small minority of people living in a few enclaves on the western seaboard known as "the *Gaeltacht*" ("GAYL-takt"). Overall fewer than 60,000 people speak Irish in preference to English, and the number grows smaller every year.

Regional Variation
Even with so few speaking Irish it still has several very distinct dialects. A native speaker from Connemara I came across thought Ulster Gaelic was a foreign language when he heard it on the radio!

Although few speak it fluently, more than a million people claim proficiency in the language. While no longer compulsory, Irish is still learned by the vast majority of children at school. Even if they do not use it in everyday life, many Irish people retain an attachment to the language and certain words and phrases still flavor everyday speech.

The Irish Care About Their Language
If you show awareness that there is an Irish language that is the repository of a marvelous literary tradition, this will definitely be appreciated.

MYTHOLOGY
Although the English rulers ignored it, Ireland has the richest canon of recorded mythology of any northern country. Just as the Greeks are proud of and familiar with their mythology, so the Irish are proud of and familiar with theirs.

Stories composed three centuries before Christ were passed on by generations of bards and written down by monks from the seventh century onward.

They were not translated into English until Lady Augusta Gregory's versions at the beginning of the twentieth century. They inspired the works of the great Irish writers of the period, especially Synge and Yeats, and were central to Ireland's rediscovery of its national identity and national pride.

The legends have been collected into four cycles. The earliest is the Mythological Cycle, or *Book of Invasions*. This tells of the invasions of six races, of which the last three have traditionally been associated with various physical types still found in Ireland. The *Firbolgs* ("FEER-bolgs") were the "bag men," the first Irish navvies, who supposedly had worked on building sites in Greece (and carried the earth away in leather bags). They were short, stocky, and dark haired—the so-called Iberian, or Spanish, Celts.

A godlike people who had magic cauldrons, magic spears, and the like, and a king with a silver hand, displaced the Firbolgs. These were the red-haired, green-eyed *Tuatha De Danann* ("TOO-ha jay DON-awn"), who were said to have originated the Druidic religion. They had strange powers, and even quite recently if fishermen saw a red-haired woman on the road they would turn back and refuse to put to sea.

But for all their magic the Tuatha De Danann were defeated by mortal men, the Milesians, or Gaels, "valiant, voluble, laughing and warlike, brown-haired, bright-eyed, skilled in the arts of peace and battle." The Tuatha De Danann were forced to live underground, coming out only at night. Ireland is full of Iron Age Barrows, or tumuli, and these were assumed to be the homes of these defeated magicians.

"The first name given the land was 'Island of Woods,' the second the 'land at the Edge of the World,' the third, in the time of the Firbolgs, was 'the Noble Island.' The fourth name was 'Eire' for she was queen of the Tuatha De Danann, the fifth and sixth names were also from queens, Fodhla and Banbha. The next name was 'Inis Fail,' the Isle of Stone; after was the 'Isle of Mists,' the next, 'Scotia' and then 'Hibernia,' and at last 'Ireland,' for Ir son of Mele, the first of his race to be buried here."

Translated from the Mythological Cycle.

The Ulster Cycle originated sometime between the third and first centuries BCE. It includes famous characters like Fergus, the exiled King of Ulster, and Queen Maeve, the proud, scheming queen behind the Cattle Raid of Cooley. But above all it is the story of Cuchulainn ("coo-KHUL-in") the champion of Ulster, who began life as a boy called Seftana. At the age of five he performed amazing heroic deeds and was seduced by hundreds of naked women. When he was six he killed the hound of Culann the Smith, and so had to take over the job of watchdog for several years. Hence his nickname the "hound of Culann"—Cuchulainn. This cycle includes the story of Deirdre of the Sorrows, which Synge dramatized.

The Fenian Cycle seems to have been written about 300 CE. By now a High King resides at Tara. The stories tell of Finn McCool, his war band, the Fianna, and his dog, Bran, who wander together all over Ireland.

"Finn and the Fianna were hunting in the mountains of Donegal when a fog overcame them. Keen-eyed Diarmud saw the white of a lime-washed cottage and there they found an old man and there was a sheep tied by the wall. The old man called to a woman below to bring food and a fine girl of exceeding beauty came and prepared a meal.

No sooner was the table laid than the sheep broke loose, upset the table and scattered the food. Finn told Conan to tie up the sheep again and Conan caught the sheep by the head. But he could not shift her though he used all his power. Then Diarmud tried and every one of them, all without success.

The old man rose from the hearth and a multitude of ashes fell from his breeches as he hobbled to the sheep, seized it by the scruff and tied it up with ease.

A further meal was prepared and Finn went to the young girl for he had a great desire to lie with her. 'Finn McCool' she said, 'you had me once and you won't have me again.' Then all the company tried but all had the same answer.

At length the girl explained. For the name of the sheep was Strength itself and it was stronger than any warrior, but the old man was Death and Death will overcome strength. And the girl herself was called 'Youth,' which all had had once but none would ever have again."

Translated from the Fenian Cycle

Finn's son Oisin and Caoilte were the only survivors of the Fianna. In old age Oisin supposedly met St. Patrick, and it is this meeting that Yeats celebrates in his *Wanderings of Oisin*.

Finally, the Historical Cycle includes legendary stories of real people and is heavily Christianized. It stretches from the third century BCE to Brian Boru, the High King who defeated the Vikings at Clontaf in 1014.

IRISH FAIRY LORE

Ireland is well-known for its fairy lore, which contains vestiges of pre-Christian traditions. In Irish, fairies are known as *sidhe* (pronounced: "shee"), a word that originally designated a mound or tumulus. In the Mythological Cycle it is recorded that, after the Milesians defeated the Tuatha De Danann, this magical race retreated from human sight beneath the ground where they became the *sidhe* and lived in *Tir Na Nog* ("Cheer na nohg"), the land of perpetual youth.

So the Tuatha De Danann became "the people" (not "the little people," many were pretty big) as the Irish called the fairies. And these resentful former rulers of the island are anything but charming.

The *Bean-sidhe* ("BANshee:" woman of the fairy) can be a young woman, a stately matron, or an old hag, or she might be a hare, a crow, or some other magic animal. Her wailing gives notice of death.

The *Pooka* ("POOK-ah") is often a dark horse with flowing mane and smoldering eyes that takes its riders, frequently drunks, on wild rides by night. In County Down he is a goblin—and there several sheaves of corn would be left standing at the end of the harvest as "the pooka's share."

The *Leprechaun* ("LEP-ruckh-awn"), who has unaccountably come to stand for all Irish fairies, is a *Leath Bhrogan*, a maker of brogues, a shoemaker.

He has a red coat with seven buttons in each row and is usually drunk. The Leprechauns took it upon themselves to guard the treasure looted by the Danes, which they store in crocks, or pots. Catch one and you may get him to hand over his crock of gold, or at least mend your shoes.

The *Moruadh* ("Merrow") wears a red cap and lives beneath the sea. Fishermen in some areas see her as a messenger of death, though several Irish families claim Merrows among their ancestors.

Other delightful fairy-folk are the *Dullaghan* ("DULLA-han"), who, headless or carrying his head, rides a black coach and throws a bowl of blood over you to tell you that you are going to die; and the *Leanaun-Shee* ("LAN-awn shee"), who likes to mate with human males. Refuse one and she will become your slave, accept her and you will become her slave and waste away, unless you can find someone to take your place as her lover.

chapter four

MAKING FRIENDS

GETTING ON WITH THE IRISH

There is a kind of magic about Ireland, in the people and the culture, but do not hope to find it at every turn. Reality, most of the time, is as ordinary here as elsewhere. Young Irish people are as likely to have a third-level education as anyone else in the English-speaking world. These days they are more likely to work on a computer than on a farm, and to dream of making a fortune from that computer rather than from finding a Leprechaun's crock of gold. They have access to the same range of goods and services, eat the same fast food, and watch the same movies and TV as everyone else does.

Nonetheless, old-fashioned values still matter. And none more than good manners. As one businessman remarked, "Good manners are good business—you don't get a second chance to make a good impression."

There is even evidence that companies are relocating to Ireland because they appreciate the warm and friendly manner. "English people tend to be more formal. They say the right thing but come across as cold." And the Irish expect the same good manners from the people they deal with.

Civil Service

Two major paging companies in Ireland automatically alter messages sent by customers to include the words "please" and "thank you." To quote the director of Pageboy: "It makes life more pleasant for our customers."

Greeting in Ireland is generally by handshake, although the continental habit of kissing ladies on the cheek has made inroads in some circles. The Irish tend to be stiffer about physical contact than, say, the Latin races, but a foreigner, especially if not Anglo-Saxon, is generally expected to be a bit more flamboyant in these matters!

Personal relations are fairly informal: more in line with American or Australian norms than north European practice. People like to get on first-name terms from the beginning. Friendships are formed quickly and visitors often find themselves invited to meet friends, or perhaps to play a round of golf or tennis.

Foreigners must be prepared sometimes to be the object of curiosity in country areas and, providing they do not stand on ceremony, will be quickly drawn into a typical rapid-fire conversation spiced with humor and imagination.

HOME LIFE

Houses and apartments in both town and country are generally modern and well appointed. Neither the picturesque thatched cottage nor the rambling great house are likely to be someone's home nowadays, and what remains of Dublin's lovely Georgian terraces often houses prestigious offices. Home life is much the same as elsewhere in the Western world, with the same comforts and facilities.

The Irish are neighborly and hospitable. Dropping by, without a prior telephone call, is accepted practice, and informal social events are not uncommon. Standing on ceremony or dressing up to call on friends would be seen as pretentious.

Because they are by nature hospitable the Irish are much more likely to invite you into their home than are the English. Should you be invited, given the high cost of alcohol in Ireland, a bottle of wine or spirits makes a welcome gift.

Get the Timing Right!

Irish social events tend to run later than in America or Britain. Guests at a dinner party, for example, should arrive twenty to thirty minutes after the appointed hour: they will not be expected precisely on time. On the other hand, leaving well before midnight could be interpreted by your hosts as a sign that their party has been deemed by you to be a failure.

Country Time

In fact the Irish generally still tend to be quite laid back about time. When a friend of mine asked when the buses came along in a rural district he got the reply, "Oh every so often with a few gaps in between."

On the subject of timing, an arrangement to meet at a pub at a particular time can be interpreted flexibly: a delay of anything up to an hour would not be considered discourteous.

The Irish attitude toward children resembles that of southern Europe. Children are accepted at social events, and if they make a nuisance of themselves it causes less concern than in some other countries. Families were relatively large until quite recently, but fertility rates are dropping fast and now two children are the norm.

It is increasingly common for both partners to work outside the home, so the pattern of family life is rapidly becoming much the same as elsewhere in the West, especially among younger people.

chapter five

CULTURAL LIFE

MUSIC, SONG, AND DANCE

The Irish love to dance, and Irish dance is central to Irish culture. Now thanks to *Riverdance* and *Lord of the Dance* it has traveled the world, but as to where it all started that, as with so much else in Ireland, is shrouded in the mists of myth and make-believe. There are those who take it back to the Druids, dancing in circles in their sacred groves of oak trees two thousand years before Christ. But the first remotely plausible evidence points to the Normans. Certainly Irish dancing was well established by the sixteenth century, when beautiful and beautifully dressed Galway girls dancing jigs impressed Sir Philip Sidney. To this day Irish dancing, unlike Scottish dancing, is chiefly the role of the womenfolk.

"Step-dancing" is essentially individual showing off. It began in competitions between dancing masters in the eighteenth century. The trick is to dance on one spot—you are supposed to be able to "dance on a plate," keeping your legs together, your hands to your sides, your face expressionless, and making as much noise as possible. The sound of the immensely complicated footwork striking the floor is known as "battering." There are step-dancing competitions all over Ireland.

A *Ceili* ("KAY-lee") is a party. A whole neighborhood would get together to dance, play music, and tell stories. Ceili dancers dance on their toes, extending legs and feet, rather than battering the floor with them. Ceili dancing, too, has its place in competitions.

"Set dances" are rather like square dances, and seem to have evolved from an old French dance— the quadrille. In summer the young people would meet up and dance at the crossroads to the music of a fiddle. Set dances involve four couples and have enormous regional variations. The Catholic Church tried to use the Public Dance Hall Act of 1935 to stamp them out, and they were only accepted into the canon of Irish dance in the 1950s.

The *ard fheis* ("ARD-esh") or dance festival is the best place to see Irish dancing, and there are hundreds of them all over Ireland. Costumes are supposed to be based on peasant dress, and those of the women are often covered in beautiful hand-embroidered Celtic designs. The men's costumes have a vaguely Scottish look with a saffron-colored kilt, short jackets, and a folded cloak draped over the shoulder.

TRADITIONAL MUSIC

Dance needs music, and much Irish traditional instrumental music has its origins in the dance—in jigs, reels, polkas, hornpipes, and such. If today dance has become a little institutionalized, music remains vastly more informal; in pubs all over Ireland, but especially in the west, you can hear players of a surprisingly high general standard. In essence the tradition of Irish music and song is oral rather than written—it is passed on from player to player, singer to singer, and father to son. Because of this, it owes comparatively little to general Western European forms. Each village would have its musicians: fiddlers, tin whistle players, accordionists, who played traditional tunes, adopting them, adapting them, making up their own songs to them about local events.

Irish music is, it has been said, "a living popular tradition," so that people forget who wrote what song. Dominic Behan once discovered songs he had written appearing in songbooks as "Anon. Traditional."

Indeed there is a long tradition of anonymous

songs stretching back into the past, or at least into the eighteenth and nineteenth centuries. Tunes are adapted, frills are added, meters change, and alternative versions of the words proliferate.

I was in a remote village pub with Tony McAuley, who is quite a well-known traditional singer, when an old fellow offered to sing us a song we wouldn't have heard. We were at first disappointed when it turned out to be "Barbara Allen," then pretty familiar on the folk circuit; but were amazed that his version was, in many respects, different from anything we had heard. It belonged to a separate oral tradition that had continued in parallel with the more familiar version.

The best-known Irish instruments are probably the small Irish harp, which has long been a national symbol (and even achieved the accolade of being adopted by Guinness as their trademark), and the *Uilleann* ("ILL-in") or elbow pipes, which are worked by bellows and have a quieter, more mellow sound than Scottish pipes. Both were originally aristocratic instruments— the pipes were far too expensive for the ordinary laborer. At one point there seemed a possibility that they would disappear, but today there are probably more Irish pipers than ever before. Ironically the version normally played was developed in Philadelphia.

In fact, the most popular instruments were the fiddle (or violin) and various forms of accordion and concertina. Guitars, of course, appear everywhere, but so do mandolins and, especially, banjos, which were brought over from America and lost one of their five strings on the voyage.

Wind instruments are the old wooden flute and the humble tin whistle (a simple metal tube with six holes and a mouthpiece like a recorder), which in the hands of accomplished players like James Galway can achieve an amazing virtuosity.

Music and the Cause

One of the best-known Northern Irish Protestant comic songs tells the story of the "Ould Orange Flute," whose owner converted to Catholicism, but the flute refused to play any but Protestant music until in the end it was burned at the stake by the priests as a heretic.

Percussion can be as simple as bones: cow rib bones or sticks clicked together like castanets, or even spoons played in the same way, but the two uniquely Irish percussion instruments are the *Bodhran* ("BOR-arn") and the Lambeg drum.

The *Bodhran* is a round frame with a goatskin stretched over it that is played with a double-ended baton that produces a stirring rapid rattle. The Lambeg is a huge drum weighing 33 pounds (15 kg) that is carried in Orange processions and whipped rather than beaten. It can be heard for miles.

Marching bands are indeed a characteristic of the North, and both the Protestant and Catholic communities have bands that accompany their parades and processions.

There is a form of singing called *Sean-nos* ("SHAN-nose") that is unaccompanied and highly ornamental and always in Irish. But, of course, it is ordinary traditional Irish song that is known throughout the world and through which Irish people have expressed their feelings, including their political aspirations. And so it continues to this day, with the two sides in Northern Ireland divided by their music and their songs.

But this sectarian use of songs to stir up Nationalist or Loyalist passions is no longer what most Irish music is about. Modern Irish music often fuses traditional with modern forms, notably in the virtuoso performances of The

Chieftains, and it has become international in the hands of world-class pop performers like Van Morrison, U2, Sinead O'Connor, the Corrs, and Ronan Keating.

LITERATURE AND THE BARDIC TRADITION

Visitors are often surprised at how interested in, and knowledgeable about, poetry and drama the ordinary people of Ireland are. Irish literature is an accepted part of normal everyday experience. It may have something to do with the Irish love of language, the fact that in old Gaelic society every village had its bard, or with the role of literature in Ireland's reassertion of its own identity.

Until nearly the end of the seventeenth century Irish literature meant literature in the Irish language. As late as 1650, bardic schools trained poets, *fili* ("Fillee"), to compose elaborate Gaelic verses. The brutal wars of the period brought this world to an end. The last, and one of the greatest, of the bards was Thurlough O'Carolan (1670–1738). It was said that at his funeral ten harpists vied to play laments for his passing.

About this time Brian Merriman was born in Limerick. An obscure schoolmaster, he was, in 1780, to write one of the most notable Gaelic poems. *Midnight Court* is a fine, bawdy, anticlerical, and feminist tale in which the poet is abducted to a court presided over by the beautiful fairy queen, Aiobheal, where women arraign men for their sexual shortcomings.

Otherwise the eighteenth century belongs to the Anglo-Irish writers, and it is surprising how many of the major English-language writers were Irishmen. Almost the only eighteenth-century playwrights whose work is still performed are George Farquhar (1678–1707), author of *The Recruiting Officer* and *The Beaux' Stratagem*, Oliver Goldsmith (1728–74), author of *She Stoops to Conquer*, and Richard Brinsley Sheridan (1751–1816), who wrote *The Rivals*, *The School for Scandal*, and *The Critic*. All three were Irish Protestants, and Farquhar and Goldsmith were educated at the Protestant Trinity College, Dublin.

So, too, was the satirist Jonathan Swift (1667–1747), Dean of St. Patrick's Cathedral, author of *Gulliver's Travels* (1726), and probably the most famous prose writer of the period. Maria Edgeworth (1767–1849) was one of the first women novelists, and her *Castle Rackrent* was an attack on the Irish landlord class to which she belonged. Inevitably most of these writers came to England to make their mark.

If Irish Protestant playwrights enlivened the eighteenth-century stage, so they did that of the late nineteenth and early twentieth centuries. Oscar Wilde (1854–1900) was the son of a Dublin

surgeon and attended Trinity College before going
to Oxford: *The Importance of Being Earnest* is
arguably the finest English comedy of manners
ever written—it is certainly the most successful.
George Bernard Shaw (1856–1950) was brought
up in a Dublin back street. The son of a drunken
wastrel father, he left school at fifteen to work for
an estate agent. At twenty he fled with his mother
to England, where he wrote a string of dramas for
the stage, most of which are still frequently
performed. He won the Nobel Prize in 1925.

The Gaelic League
However, while Wilde and Shaw were making
their names in England, great things were
happening in Ireland. In 1893 the Gaelic League
was founded to assert the Irishness of the Irish
people. The Irish language was to be learned, Irish
dances, Irish poetry and song, Irish mythology,
even Irish clothes, were encouraged. Its moving
spirit was a delightful man called Douglas Hyde,
the son of a Protestant clergyman and another
Trinity College graduate.

It would be hard to overestimate the
importance of the Gaelic League on the future of
Ireland, even though it was founded by middle-
class Protestant intellectuals. Michael Collins, as
hardheaded a man of action as ever Ireland
produced, called it the "greatest event . . . in the

whole history of the nation," since it "did more than any other movement to restore the national pride, honor, and self respect."

Hyde went on to be Professor of Modern Irish, a concept that could not have existed without him, at University College, Dublin, and, much to his own surprise, first President of the Irish Republic. His genius lay in reclaiming not just Gaelic literature but the poetry of the proverbs and everyday speech of the Irish countryman.

Above all it was William Butler Yeats (1865–1939), the grandson of a Protestant clergyman, whose work inspired the modern renaissance in Irish writing. In his own poetry and plays Yeats, who was awarded the Nobel Prize in 1923, drew heavily on the Irish mythological past and so made the Irish people aware and proud of the richness of their birthright.

Yeats also got together with other idealists, like Lady Augusta Gregory, the widow of an Anglo-Irish landowner, to form the Irish National Theatre Society. In 1907 they opened the Abbey Theatre in Dublin with *The Playboy of the Western World* by John Millington Synge. While Synge's background was similar to theirs, he had lived on

speech and culture of the islanders. Because it did
not romanticize them, *The Playboy* caused an
uproar on the first night.

Yeats and Lady Gregory belonged to the Celtic
Revival, or "Celtic Twilight" as it was sometimes
called, and wrote plays set in the mythological
past. But the Abbey's real future lay elsewhere.
Sean O'Casey was a Protestant, but otherwise very
different from the "Celtic Twilight" group. He had
worked as a laborer, was a convinced socialist, and
had been a member of the rebel Irish Citizens
Army. His great Dublin Trilogy—*The Shadow of a
Gunman, Juno and the Paycock,* and *The Plough
and the Stars*—was about the Easter Rising, the
"Tan War," and the Civil War. Though put on by
the Abbey in the 1920s when wounds were still
raw, they pulled no punches in condemning the
men of violence and speaking out for
compassion. The plays are full of humor but their
message is the stuff of tragedy. As Juno prays
when she learns her son has been executed by his
comrades, "Blessed Virgin, where were you when
me darlin' son was riddled with bullets? Sacred
heart of Jesus, take away our hearts o'stone and
give us hearts o' flesh!" It is a line much quoted in
Northern Ireland today.

Juno was hissed when it was first performed,
and there was a full-scale riot when *The Plough*

and the Stars dared to criticize the Easter Rising—whose banner carried a Plough and Stars.

The Gate, Micheal Mac Liammoir's theater, founded in 1928, staged European classics, but The Abbey continued to mount controversial plays into the 1950s, with Brendan Behan's *The Hostage*, about the IRA, of which he had been a member, and later with Tom Murphy's *The Famine* in 1964. Recently it has maintained its reputation for realistic, unromantic pictures of Irish life with Billy Roche's trilogy about his home town of Wexford, and for controversy with John Breen's *Hinterland*, a thinly disguised attack on the former Prime Minister Charles Haughey.

But not all playwrights come from near Dublin. John B. Keane lives in Listowel in County Kerry, and well-known plays such as *Big Maggie* and *The Field*, were premiered by an amateur group in Cork.

IRISH NOVELISTS

Of the hundreds of Irish novelists there is room to mention only a few. Edna O'Brien's *Country Girls* trilogy draws on her experience of being brought up in an "enclosed, fervid, and bigoted" village and educated in a convent. John McGahern's novels also recall the experience of being raised in the countryside, while Maeve Binchy is equally at home writing about village life and about young

Irish women in London. Frank McCourt's best-seller, *Angela's Ashes*, describes his hard life as a child in Limerick, and Roddy Doyle's novels about life on a Dublin housing estate combine popular appeal with a serious analysis of Irish society.

Then there are the short-story writers, from Frank O'Connor and Sean O'Faolain to William Trevor, and poets like Patrick Kavanagh and the Northerner Louis MacNeice.

Flann O'Brien wrote equally well in English and Irish. His comic English-language masterpieces, *At Swim Two Birds* and *The Third Policeman*, are among the few works worthy of comparison with *Ulysses*.

Which brings up James Joyce. *Ulysses*, published in1922, is probably the most influential novel ever written. Every chapter is in a different style as, in imitation of the travels of Odysseus in Homer's *Odyssey*, it traces the travels of Leopold Bloom around Dublin on a single day in 1904.

Samuel Beckett worked with Joyce, and his plays, of which the most famous is *Waiting for Godot*, have had the same profound effect on theatrical writing across the world as Joyce has had on prose.

The Milesians, having conquered the Tuatha de Danaan, sent a harpist south and a bard to the north. And to this day, so people say, the musicians hail from the South and the poets from the North.

Whether this is true or not, there has been an amazing flowering of literature in the North. In the sixties a galaxy of talent emerged, including the novelist Maurice Leitch, the playwright Brian Friel, and the poets Michael Longley, Derek Mahon, and Seamus Heaney. The son of a small farmer, Heaney is currently Boyston Professor of Rhetoric and Poetry at Harvard. He was Professor of Poetry at Oxford from 1989 to 1994, and in 1995 was awarded the Nobel Prize for Literature.

These were followed by a second wave of younger writers, the poets Tom Paulin, Ciaran Carson, and Paul Muldoon, the current Oxford Professor of Poetry, and the playwrights Ann Devlin, Frank McGuinness, and Marie Jones.

FILM

Stones in His Pockets, based on Marie Jones's novel *A Night in November,* is a reminder that the 1990s saw a series of films about Ireland, starting with *The Field* in 1991. Many had themes based on the Troubles: films like *Patriot Games*, with Harrison Ford, *Some Mother's Son* and *Cal* with Helen Mirren, *The Boxer* and *In the Name of the Father* with Daniel Day-Lewis, and *The Crying Game* with Stephen Rea. Others were simply about life in Ireland, like the film version of Maeve Binchy's *Circle of Friends, Widows Peak* with Mia Farrow, set in the 1920s, and the delightful homegrown comedy *Waking Ned Divine*, about a dead lottery winner and a whole village of schemers. Liam Neeson's biographical film *Michael Collins* came out in 1996.

FESTIVALS

Poetry in Irish and English, drama, jazz, film, dance, and traditional music are all good excuses for a festival or *feis* ("FESH") or *Flea cheoil* ("FLAH hyowl"—a music festival), and Ireland has an awful lot of festivals, many of which seem to take place in Galway. Here is a small, not especially representative, selection:

February: Newtonabbey Arts Festival; Castlereagh Verbal Arts Festival; Cookstown Drama Festival; Ballymoney Drama Festival.

March: St. Patrick's Day (17th), Drama festival, Enniskillen; Limerick International Band Festival.

April: Irish Grand National; Dublin Film Festival; Cuirt International Festival of Poetry and Literature.

May: *Flea na gCuach* ("FLAH-na-Guarch"), the Cuckoo festival; Ericsson All Ireland Drama Festival; Early Music Festival in Galway; Blues in the Bay Festival at Warren Point.

June: Cork Midsummer Festival; Irish Derby, International Organ and Choral Festival, Dublin;

Bloomsday Festival (16th)—the day in 1904 when James Joyce sent Leopold Bloom wandering round Dublin in *Ulysses*.

July: Galway Arts Festival; O'Carolan Summer School.

August: Wagner Festival, Limerick; "Gathering of the boats at Kinvara;" All-Ireland Hurling Finals; "Rose of Tralee"; Puck Fair.

September: Lisdoonvarna Matchmaking Festival; Dublin Jazz Festival; Gaelic Football final; Dublin Theatre Festival; Galway Oyster Festival.

October: International Arts Festival for children, Galway; Wexford Opera Festival; Cork Guinness Jazz Festival; Belfast Festival at Queen's University.

November: film festival in Northern Ireland.

The Puck Fair merits a touch more detail. It is a totally pagan occasion that takes place on three successive days in August, generally the 10th, 11th, and 12th, at Killorglin on the River Laune. The three days are known as Gathering Day, Binding Day, and Scattering Day. The key event, and what makes the whole thing so outrageously pre-Christian, is the crowning with flowers of a very obviously male, or puck, goat on the first day in the presence of 30,000 celebrating spectators.

TIME OUT

FOOD AND EATING OUT

The Irish diet is broadly similar to that of Britain. Continental Europe has exercised an increasing influence and, as in Britain, has done much to bring about a new focus on quality, choice, and service.

Restaurants and Pub Food

Nothing symbolizes the transformation of Irish life in the last twenty years more than the proliferation of restaurants and eating establishments of all kinds, many noted for their high quality and some for equally high prices.

In Dublin it is possible to sample most of the world's cuisines. Temple Bar, Dame Street, and the Grafton Street and Duke Street areas are particularly rich in restaurants. Mexican, Italian, and Indian can all be found, as well as fine seafood restaurants; Chinese restaurants abound, as do chains of Kebab and Middle Eastern food shops. There are even, despite the Irish fondness for meat, plenty of vegetarian restaurants.

For local dishes and fine plain cooking, Irish pubs offer good food and good value, especially at lunchtime. One of the most famous Dublin pubs is Davy Byrne's in Duke Street—famous because it appears in James Joyce's *Ulysses*. In a typically "Joycean" passage, Leopold Bloom drops into Davy Byrne's for a sandwich of gorgonzola cheese and mustard, washed down with a glass of Burgundy.

> "*Mr Bloom ate his strips of sandwich, fresh clean bread, with relish of disgust, pungent mustard, the feety savour of green cheese. Sips of his wine soothed his palate. Not logwood that. Tastes fuller this weather with the chill off . . .*"
>
> **James Joyce, *Ulysses***

Incidentally Irish pubs, like New York bars, are usually named after the proprietor. The oldest pub in Dublin is called "The Brazen Head," but such fanciful names are rare.

Continental-style cafes are mushrooming in towns throughout the island, contributing to the evolution of a whole new lifestyle. Most serve light food, and some serve alcohol as well.

Traditional Irish breakfasts include bacon, egg, sausage, tomatoes, white and black puddings (made from pig's blood), soda and potato bread, all followed by toast and washed down with tea. If you are staying at a farmhouse, with luck, everything will be local produce. If you are staying in town, remember the Irish are not famous for being early risers, so that by the time your breakfast arrives you will probably be hungry enough to eat it.

In Dublin, with the spread of health consciousness among the growing middle class, the norm is now likely to be a light breakfast and a snack lunch with the main meal in the evening.

To Tip or Not to Tip?

Tipping is expected in hotels and restaurants, with 10–15 percent being the norm. The percentage charge to the check has been introduced in some establishments, sometimes leaving the customer with no option except to add even more to the tip!

English-style afternoon tea has never really been part of Irish life, though some hotels do serve it. In Northern Ireland, however, "High Tea," served from about 5:30 p.m. onward, is something very special and frequently the main meal of the day. There is tea, of course, but with it come scones, cakes, several types of bread, including currant or raisin bread, cold meat or a hot dish, a grilled or fried fish.

Sometimes Ulster hotels do not even serve dinner in the evening, and where they do it can be expensive.

In the Republic, at least in the towns, you should have no trouble finding restaurants that serve evening meals, and many pubs serve them. Be warned though, that these places can close quite early, and pubs in particular are often unwilling to serve food after 8:30 or 9:00 a.m. when the bartenders want to get down to their proper business of selling drinks.

Sundays

The explosion of fast-food restaurants means you can eat cheaply most hours of the day or night in the Republic. Basic shopping on a Sunday is rarely a problem either, as the southern Irish do not have a rigid Sabbatarian culture (Irish games, for example, are played on Sundays). Be warned though, the same is not true of Northern Ireland. In Northern Ireland the pubs and almost all shops are closed on Sundays. Going out to a restaurant for Sunday lunch is something of an institution, and since comparatively few places are open it is always advisable to book. Many restaurants that open Sunday lunchtime are closed in the evening.

Service

Away from the fast-food outlets service can be leisurely. And unfortunately attempting to hurry

the Irish waiter or waitress can be
counterproductive. Not that they will argue with
you. If you complain they will apologize and find
some plausible excuse. But the resentment at what
they see as your impatience can come out in making
you wait even longer. The Irish themselves, while
they may grumble privately, tend to suffer in silence.

Irish Food and Irish Dishes
The glory of Irish country food is the quality of
local produce, and it is always worth sampling
local specialities like Limerick ham or
Galway oysters (served with
buttered brown bread
and Guinness).

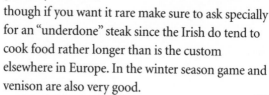

Salmon, fresh or
smoked locally, and local
lamb are the other
famous specialities of
the west. Irish beef is
generally excellent,
though if you want it rare make sure to ask specially
for an "underdone" steak since the Irish do tend to
cook food rather longer than is the custom
elsewhere in Europe. In the winter season game and
venison are also very good.

Old habits die hard and everywhere in rural
Ireland no meal is complete without a serving
of potato.

Indeed, food often comes with two different forms of potato. Boiled potatoes, usually in their skins, will be served together with roasted potatoes, mashed potatoes, or even French fries. Except in the main urban centers salads are generally unimaginative and disappointing—though like so much else in Ireland, tastes are changing rapidly.

Irish Generosity
Irish portions tend toward the generous—generosity, in Irish *flathuil* ("FLA-hooal"), is a much-admired trait in Irish life—even in international hotels, but no offense will be taken if food is left.

All too often now you are served standard sliced bread. Yet proper Irish bread is world-famous, and Northern Irish bread is regarded throughout Ireland as the best of all. Soda bread is made of stone-ground wheat flour baked on a griddle, and, instead of yeast, bicarbonate of soda and buttermilk are used. "Baps" are usually soft rolls, while "bannocks" are a soda bread made from oatmeal, and like many of the Northern Irish themselves were originally Scottish. "Barmbrack" is a spiced bread served at high tea—and, of course, there is potato bread.

Freshwater fish, notably excellent salmon and trout, have always been a valued part of the Irish menu, but until quite recently this was not the case with seafood, which many people thought "rots the brain."

Today, though, seafood is an Irish speciality, and especially in the west. Fine West Coast lobsters, scallops, mussels, and sole can all be found in the restaurants of Galway or exported to those of Dublin, and they are generally simply and deliciously cooked.

Knives and Forks

Table manners in Ireland follow the English convention of holding the knife in the right hand and the fork in the left. The American practice of changing the fork over to the right hand to eat with after the food has been cut up is not usual.

While Ireland has not evolved as comprehensive a cuisine as, say, France or Italy, or even, let's face it, Malta, there are some distinctive dishes well worth trying. These, of course, usually involve potatoes.

"Boxty" is a sort of potato pancake using both mashed and ordinary boiled potatoes (sometimes with an egg added) fried in bacon fat.

"Colcannon" is a type of mashed potato incorporating cabbage and onion, often served at

Hallowe'en. The simpler version called "Champ" is mashed potato with spring onions.

"Dublin Coddle" is a sort of thick stew in which sausages and bacon are interlayered with onions and, yes, potatoes, cooked in a ham stock.

It should not be confused with Irish stew, which is made with cheap cuts of lamb, carrots, onions, potatoes, any other root vegetables available, and pearl barley.

"Bacon and Cabbage" is just that—and delicious if the bacon is home-cured and the cabbage is not overcooked.

Finally, to bring us on to drinks, two dishes involving Guinness. Beef in Guinness is Ireland's answer to *coq au vin*, and Guinness Cake is a rich fruitcake additionally flavored with Guinness.

DRINKING AND PUBS

The pub is the great focus of Irish social life. In the countryside the pub sometimes doubles as the local grocer's shop and, with the church, is the center of village life. The Irish pub, whether in the great cities, in towns, or in the countryside, is an egalitarian place where all classes and nationalities can mingle and enjoy the art of conversation over a few drinks. There is an easiness, a sense of bonhomie that, quite apart from the drink, can prove intoxicating.

In Dublin restaurants and pubs a good selection of wines are as available as they were in 1904 when Mr. Bloom drank his glass of Burgundy in Davy Byrne's. But elsewhere, particularly in rural areas, this is not always the case.

Unlike England, Ireland does not produce a great number of local beers. There are two drinks, however, that are specifically Irish, and ordering these will earn you your host's approval.

One is whiskey. The Irish insist that the first whiskey (which they spell with an "e") was Irish, not Scotch. The word is a corruption of the Gaelic *uisce beatha*, which means "water of life," and this, they say, was invented by Irish monks in the sixth century. Certainly the world's oldest (legal) distillery is at Bushmills on the Antrim coast, where they have been making whiskey since 1608.

Each Irish whiskey has a distinct taste, so people tend to order their favorite by name. Apart from Bushmills, other well-known whiskeys are John Jameson of Dublin, John Powers and Paddy of Cork, and Locke's of Kilbeggan. Tullamore Dew, which has a sweeter, smoother taste, is often drunk as an aperitif.

Poteen

They might not admit it but some of these distillers had their origin in the illegal distilling of *poteen* ("po-cheen"), a clear, very alcoholic spirit. In the early nineteenth century there were said to be 2,000 illicit distillers in Ireland, though I've no idea who counted them. There are indeed still plenty of illegal poteen makers in the countryside, but it is not recommended that you try their wares. If you are desperate to taste poteen, the law was changed in 1997 to enable it to be brewed legally, so legal, hygienically distilled poteen is now available in some liquor stores.

And of course there is Irish coffee—hot, sweet, black coffee with a good measure of Irish whiskey and topped with whipped cream. Not exactly an ancient Irish tipple—it was said to have been invented by a barman at Shannon airport in the 1950s—but a luxurious ending to any meal.

But it is Guinness, a brand of dark beer made with dark roasted barley, that is synonymous with Ireland around the world and is seen as the national drink—though in fact there are other, similar, dark beers. Beamish and Murphy's, for instance, both have devoted followings.

In Ireland you will often hear Guinness called "porter" or "stout." Porter was invented not in Ireland but in London. It got its name from being drunk by porters, and was a particularly cheap beer that used dark roasted barley to cover up any imperfections drifting in the glass. Many of the porters who drank it were Irish Catholics, so the idea got back to Dublin where in 1759 Arthur Guinness took over an abandoned brewery in St. James' Gate. In Dublin "porter" was later called "plain" to distinguish it from proper Guinness.

Later, hearing of a much improved version that the porters at London's Covent Garden market had taken to drinking, Arthur Guinness tried his hand at this stronger, or "stout" version. So, just as "Scotch whisky" was invented in Ireland, so the origin of Ireland's favorite beverage is actually London, England!

Soon Guinness spread all over the world, and the Guinness family became a force to be reckoned with in Irish Society. They were especially involved in charitable work.

The Goodness of Guinness

When the writer Brendan Behan became famous he was taken up by the Guinness family. One day they were discussing the good works the family had done, and one of them said to the writer, "The Guinness family have done a lot for the people of Ireland." "True," said Brendan, "but that's nothing to what the people of Ireland have done for the Guinness family!"

To watch an Irish barman carefully pouring a draught Guinness can be quite an experience. It may take up to five minutes, after which it is smoothed off with a special implement that looks like ivory but is in fact plastic. You would think it was a sort of religious ritual going back to the days of the Druids. In fact draught Guinness was introduced in 1961, prior to which it was only available in bottles.

One reason for the special taste of Irish stout and whiskey is the marvelous quality of Irish water, and this has been the case for many years. Spanish sailors from the Armada fleet who were shipwrecked on the Irish coast in 1588 are said to have so much admired the sweetness of the water that they "could not understand why the Irish should want to drink anything else!"

A word of warning: if you go to a pub and ask for a Guinness or a lager you will automatically be served a pint (about half a liter)—if you want a half-pint, ask for "a glass," or a "half."

Don't Forget to Stand your Round!

The Irish are a naturally generous people and, although the "round" system (buying a drink for all in your company) is nothing like as prevalent as it was a generation ago, it is still an important fact of pub culture. If you have accepted a drink from an individual or as part of a round, you should reciprocate. No one will say anything if you do not, but they may not be pleased to see you the following evening. Similarly if you are smoking, you should offer the packet around (again, no comment will be passed if you decide not to; you will simply come across as mildly antisocial).

No Pub Tips

If you are buying drinks in Irish pubs, except possibly where you are seated at a table and there is a waiter, you should not leave a tip. The English practice of offering the bar staff a drink is not widespread either.

Licensing laws in Ireland are broadly similar to those in England, and visiting Americans or continental Europeans might regard them as restrictive. Pubs close at 11:30 p.m. in the summer and at 11:00 p.m. in the winter.

The Irish Don't Drink—That Much!

Nobody works harder to promote an image of wild excess surrounding Irish pub culture than the Irish themselves. However, the sober statistics tell another story: the Irish are among the most modest consumers of alcohol in the world. There are a number of reasons for this. The Irish are slow drinkers and can nurse a pint, or a whiskey and water, for a very long time. Then the Irish do not as a rule drink every day, or with their meals. And the Catholic temperance movement, the Pioneers, is quite influential.

A reflection of the changes in Irish society and attitudes is the way, in the last thirty years, that Irish pubs have been transformed from essentially male-dominated drinking haunts to social centers where both sexes are equally welcome.

There is a wide variety of Irish pubs. In Dublin there are poets' pubs; in some rural areas Gaelic games may be the main topic of conversation; and one Dublin pub has given its name to a school of economics! But above all there are singing pubs and musical pubs where you can hear traditional songs and traditional music, and stand up and sing yourself if you feel so inclined.

So we come to the useful but elusive concept of the *craic*. This is pronounced "crack," but rest easy: the phrase "the *craic* is good," in a certain pub, does not refer to the high quality of the crack cocaine! What it actually means is a bit obscure. Certainly it involves good conversation, but it also implies having a good time when the drink is flowing well, and maybe the music is flowing well. Dancing may even be involved.

Suffice it to say that an Irishman can give no higher praise than that the "*craic* was good." And Irish pubs are the best place to find good *craic*.

THE SPORTING LIFE

With the growth of corporate entertainment in Ireland, business visitors are increasingly likely to find themselves invited to sports events since sports play an important part in national life. And playing golf or going fishing is a good way to meet the Irish in an unselfconscious way.

The Irish love to watch sports. Dublin's main thoroughfares can be deserted when almost everyone is watching a key international match. Similarly the whole country will take a great interest in, and maybe gamble a few Euros on, high-profile horse races.

Horse Racing

Involvement in horse racing conveys high status in Ireland, and betting on the outcome is acceptable at all levels of society. Indeed, while the Irish have a love of all forms of sports, they love horses in particular. In the horse-breeding counties of Tipperary, Limerick, and Kildare it is said that only God takes precedence over the horse. That's understandable, since mares from all over the world are brought to Ireland for breeding, and the bloodstock industry brings in about E100 million a year—and the profits are tax-free to the bloodstock owners!

Something of the Irish people's passion for horse racing is conveyed by the fact that there are twenty-eight racecourses in Ireland, almost all in the Republic, attended by more than a million people in the course of a year. The classic flat races, such as the Irish Derby in June, are held at the Curragh in County Kildare. The flat racing season is from mid-March to early November, but National Hunt racing (steeplechasing) over fences, which the Irish claim to have invented, takes place all year. The great classic steeplechase is the Irish Grand National on Easter Monday at Fairyhouse in County Dublin. Probably the most

enjoyable event in the racing calendar is the
Punchestown festival in March.

Dog Racing

Dog, or greyhound, racing is horse racing's
proletarian cousin. It began in Belfast in 1927 and
remains especially popular in the North. There is
even a pub named after the legendary Irish
greyhound, Master McGrath, in Belfast—and, for
that matter, a statue to him in Kildare.

Soccer

Soccer is not a major sport in the Republic.
Nevertheless when Ireland played Germany in
the 2002 World Cup, 95 percent of companies
extended their lunch breaks and nearly half gave
staff the afternoon off to watch. The Irish team is
largely made up of men who play across the
water in English or Scottish clubs, and Irish fans
all too often prefer to watch these matches on
British television rather than go out and
support one of the twelve teams in the Irish
professional league.

Northern Ireland is another matter. Here
soccer is *the* spectator sport. Being Northern
Ireland, team affiliation tends to be on sectarian
lines rather as it is in Glasgow, where Celtic
(which has a large following in Northern Ireland)
is the Catholic team, and Rangers the Protestant.

Rugby

Rugby is largely confined to the middle classes, but when Ireland is playing an international match the whole country is glued to its television sets. Ireland has won the "triple crown" six times, though not since 1985, but has come last more than thirty times. Nevertheless they have had some excellent players, and Fergus Slattery and Willie John McBride, who each won more than sixty caps, became national heroes.

Dress Codes

The casual visitor need not worry unduly about dress at sports events, but the recipients of hospitality should dress fairly formally. A suit or sports jacket, with stout shoes such as brogues would be appropriate for men, while women will find they need to dress with a degree of fashion consciousness so as not to be out of place among their Irish counterparts. For those with a budget to match, wearing an outfit from an internationally recognized Irish designer, such as Paul Costello, would be a definite plus. A major sports event may be tied in with a formal social occasion, such as a ball, where a tuxedo and equivalent dress for women is a requirement. Invitees should check this point out in advance.

Gaelic Football and Hurling

The most popular sports in Ireland are the Irish games of Gaelic Football and Hurling. These can attract huge crowds—the highest recorded attendance at an All-Ireland Gaelic Football match was 90,556 in 1961.

Croke Park near Dublin, the headquarters of Gaelic games, is being rebuilt as an 80,000-plus stadium with forty-six hospitality suites containing lavish corporate entertainment facilities, so it is likely that an increasing number of business and other visitors will be invited to games there. In any case, your Irish hosts are likely to be impressed, and even moved, if you show an interest in these sports since they are an essential part of the national ethos. Their revival was a key element in Ireland's rediscovery of itself as a special and unique culture.

Hurling is the true game of the Gael and very ancient—it was played well before St. Patrick brought Christianity to Ireland. Hurling was the sport of the heroes of Irish mythology: Finn McCool and Cuchulainn both played it. The modern game has teams of fifteen players and is fast, skillful, and very dangerous—its original name was *baire boise*, or imitation warfare! It is dangerous because it is played with a heavy "hurley" that looks a little like a hockey stick— though be warned; never compare it with hockey to an Irishman! The blade of the hurley is wide enough for a clever player to balance the ball on it. The goalposts resemble rugby goalposts and points are scored either by hitting the ball over the crossbar or under it. A goal is worth three points.

The revival of Gaelic sports was very much part of the nationalist movement. The Gaelic Athletic Association (GAA) is an amateur sporting association founded in 1884 by the Celtic Revival movement. Its first president was Dr. T. W. Croke, Catholic bishop of Cashel, after whom the main stadium, Croke Park, near Dublin, is named.

Games take place on Sundays—the only free day the Irish agricultural laborer had, and a day when sports were prohibited by the British authorities. Today the great event of the Irish sporting calendar is the All-Ireland Gaelic Football final at Croke Park on the third Sunday in September, when the winners are presented with the Sam Maguire cup.

Gaelic Football resembles Hurling in that it has teams of fifteen players, and the same sort of goalposts, where you can score by putting the ball either over or under the crossbar. The ball, which is round like a small soccer ball, can be either kicked or thrown, with one point for putting it over the bar and three for putting it in the net. It is a little like American football, but most resembles Australian football.

Within six months of the GAA's foundation there were clubs all over Ireland, and today Gaelic Football is played by 250,000 people, Hurling by 100,000, and its female version, "Camogie," by 50,000 women.

The atmosphere at an intercounty match is always one of good will, and the all-Ireland football final in particular is a marvelous occasion. Everyone is there: bishops, priests, farmers, laborers, shopkeepers, and corner boys. Bands play and the President of Ireland throws in the ball. Spectators warmly applaud good playing by each side, and there is none of the hostility between opposing supporters that can make English football matches so disagreeable.

Golf

The number of golf courses is, in relation to the size of population, among the highest in the

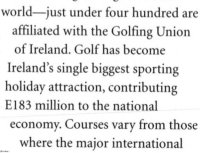

world—just under four hundred are affiliated with the Golfing Union of Ireland. Golf has become Ireland's single biggest sporting holiday attraction, contributing E183 million to the national economy. Courses vary from those where the major international tournaments are held to a small friendly course in the west where you may have to wave goats away from the green.

Other Sports
Other participation sports like tennis and badminton are well catered for. Dress codes for these sports are much the same as in Britain or America.

Fishing
With so much water in and around Ireland, and because Ireland's rivers and lakes are the purest in Europe, Ireland both North and South is something of a paradise for anglers. The Fisheries Board stocks many lakes with rainbow trout, which are not indigenous to Ireland and will not breed there. The true Irish fish are the salmon and the lovely little brown trout, which have an honored place in Irish culture and myth.

While coarse fishing and sea trout fishing are traditional, sea fishing is a relatively new sport. The warm waters of the Gulf Stream mean that fish such as the shark or the blue fin tuna have a far longer season here than elsewhere at these latitudes.

Poachers Turned Gamekeepers

It is characteristic of Irish morality that where I was staying in Donegal the poaching of salmon was considered perfectly moral—after all, the fishing rights were owned by the local landlord who did not even live in the area. But you had to play fair and use a rod and line; anyone who used a net was an outcast. And as for dropping a small stick of dynamite in the river and killing fish that way—that was virtually a hanging offense.

Road Bowling

There is one sport that is unique to two areas— West Cork in the deep south and Antrim in the far north. I came across it while quietly wandering down a country road in County Cork. Suddenly I was horrified to see a vicious-looking steel ball come hurtling toward me. I had discovered Road Bowling. It is played on Sundays when the Irish roads are even quieter than usual. Intercounty games take place, but they have to be between Cork and Antrim, so the players have to travel the length of Ireland from Antrim in the Protestant North to Cork, the

heartland of the Republican South. Neither the
Garda nor the Northern Irish police would
dream of arresting these sportsmen for misuse of
the public highway!

chapter seven

BUSINESS BRIEFING

The Irish economy has two distinct sectors: the indigenous, much of which is still related to agriculture and the traditional industries, and the newer, largely high-tech, sector, developed mostly with foreign capital. This distinction is not as pronounced as it used to be, thanks to the emergence of Irish entrepreneurs in the newer sector. Currently Ireland is the second-largest exporter of computer software in the world, after the U.S.A., and attracts 25 percent of all investment in electronics in the European Union.

THE ECONOMY: THE REPUBLIC
The Irish economy is dependent on trade and tourism, with a healthy growth rate averaging 9 percent between 1995 and 2000. Agriculture

takes up about 70 percent of the land and 13 percent of the workforce, chiefly dairy and beef cattle, sheep, pigs, and poultry. The main crops are flax, oats, wheat, turnips, potatoes, sugar beet, and barley. There is a flourishing meat and fish export sector.

Industry, however, which includes food processing, accounts for nearly 80 percent of exports and 40 percent of the GDP (Gross Domestic Product, defined as the sum of all incomes earned from productive activity). Agriculture accounts for only about 7 percent of the GDP and 9 percent of exports.

Light industry predominates, and the main exports are electronic equipment, in particular computers and all things related to them; also luxury textiles like lace and linen, beverages such as Guinness and Irish whiskey, Waterford Crystal, pharmaceuticals, plastics, and handicrafts.

About 35 percent of exports go to the U.K. and 40 percent of imports come from the U.K.; 12 percent or so of exports go to Germany, 11 percent to the U.S., and nearly 8 percent to France.

Foreign penetration of business in Ireland is the highest in Europe. Over 900 foreign-owned firms control 50 percent of the total turnover and employ 40 percent of the workforce. Most foreign companies are British, American, and German, but there are a number of Japanese. Both foreign and Irish firms benefit from a traditionally state-led economy. There are government employment schemes, European Union and government subsidies, and tax breaks. There is also considerable direct government ownership.

Tourism is still one of Ireland's fastest-growing industries. Overseas visitor numbers have grown from 2.3 million in 1997 to more than 5 million today. A survey in 1997 indicated that 57 percent came from Britain and 16 percent from North America.

Within a generation, and especially in the last decade of the twentieth century, Eire has jumped from being one of the poorest to one of the richest EU member states. This remarkable economic performance was underpinned by a "Programme for Competitiveness and Work," essentially a broad "social contract" between the major social partners, which helped make the trade (U.S. "labor") unions associates rather than adversaries in their relations with capital. Visitors dealing with unions should start by seeking cooperation with them.

THE ECONOMY: NORTHERN IRELAND

The largest single occupation is, somewhat surprisingly, farming: proportionately more cereals are grown than in the Republic, but livestock and dairy products still predominate, and potatoes are also important. As in the South most farmers own their farms, though many are too small to provide a living: the average size of the 25,000 largest farms is only 72 acres, half the U.K. average. The livestock has an excellent health record: the beef is mainly exported to Britain, lamb goes to France, and a quarter of all the U.K.'s bacon comes from Ulster.

Manufacturing output in Northern Ireland has increased significantly over the last five years and at a faster rate than that of the U.K. as a whole.

Belfast linen is world famous, but other textiles are also important. Heavy industry, notably shipbuilding, is based in Belfast but is having a difficult time at the moment, though other forms of engineering are doing better. Other industries include food processing, electronic goods, papermaking, and furniture.

INTERNATIONALISM

As the British, Americans, and Germans are the largest investors in Ireland, visiting businesspeople should find that dealing with their Irish counterparts in the foreign-funded areas of the economy is not fundamentally different from elsewhere. The workforce is young, computer literate, and professional. Even in the traditional industries, where the approach might seem more relaxed, the law of the bottom line applies as ruthlessly as anywhere else. All sectors of the economy have had to survive the global forces that have weeded out so many sunset industries in the last twenty years.

BUSINESS ETIQUETTE

The Irish dress formally for business meetings. Even so, the human touch remains vital. People shake hands on meeting and departure; eye contact is expected, and the old rural tradition of indirectness still survives. It is normal to exchange a few pleasantries before getting down to business since establishing a warm relationship is considered important. An unassuming courteousness is appreciated, though excessive politeness, especially to a boss, is frowned on—as is excessive praise!

Aggressive sales techniques are unlikely to be appreciated, especially in country areas. Take things slowly and allow your professional relationship to develop as your Irish counterpart comes to know and trust you. The use of first names is standard practice. Exchanging business cards is not routine, so a request for a card can be a sign of genuine interest.

Manners Makyth Money

With regard to doing business in Ireland, Lisa Muza Grotts, the Director of a San Francisco-based consultancy firm says categorically, "It all comes down to 'please,' 'May I?' 'I am sorry,' 'Excuse me,' and 'Thank you.' Each time you omit one of these terms you are hurting feelings and profits."

WOMEN IN BUSINESS

There is no legal discrimination at any level, but as Mary Robinson, the first woman President, remarked, the patriarchal male-dominated Catholic Church wields a lot of influence, and women may still be paid less than men for doing the same job.

The masculine pronoun still rules so there are "businessmen" not "businesspeople" and "chairmen" not "chairs." "Mrs." and "Miss" still tend to be used in preference to "Ms." For visiting businesswomen, being well dressed is important, but so is not being ostentatious, or indeed over familiar in manner!

Men still tend to think of women as secretaries and personal assistants, so if you are the boss or a senior executive it is important that you establish your business credentials and position discreetly but clearly.

MANAGEMENT STYLE

In many businesses the boss is the key decision-maker and authority figure; but this may be masked by an atmosphere of informal communication in which instructions are often presented in the form of polite requests.

Irish business admires eccentrics, rebels, and artists, but in practice tends to be conservative, especially when it comes to making decisions. As in the U.K. there is a tendency for decision-making to be on an "ad hoc" short-term basis, in preference to long-term planning.

MEETINGS, NEGOTIATIONS, AND COMMUNICATION

Meetings are generally welcoming, warm, and friendly. A "down-to-earth" approach is appreciated. Agendas are not inviolate, and there is a certain resistance to structure and routine. Ideas are as important as facts, so by all means be imaginative—Irish businesses embrace creativity and are always looking for new ways to approach problems and tasks. But a caveat: such daring is not always followed up. The way things are done can be regarded as just as important as getting a result.

Some Dos and Don'ts

Do not try to shortcut established processes—go with them, sell your ideas gently—however much you may know you are right! Justify what you say in an objective, reasonable way.

Do not precipitate confrontations. Be tactful: it pays to start from a position of apparent agreement and compliance. Open dissent is rare so be prepared to read between the lines; responses can be cryptic! A period of silence in conversation is likely to signal problems.

In presenting your case, an informal, conversational style usually works best. The quality and style of your language will be significant, and humor, anecdotes, and jokes are appreciated—but avoid sarcasm.

Also avoid too much technical language, too many visual aids, etc. To prove points rely on simple practical facts and verbal fluency.

Do not be fooled by an apparent dreaminess; the Irish are cunning businessmen.

"*The Irish are a very spiritual people and the longer it takes you to pay them the more spiritual they become.*"
Conor Cruise O'Brien

There are no words for "yes" and "no" in true Gaelic, and perhaps this is why the Irish do not like to say "yes" or "no" outright. Be prepared for noncommittal answers . . . maybe, perhaps . . . It is not a good idea to force decisions, as this may damage relationships.

TEAMS AND TEAMWORK

Team members work cooperatively, combining their skills, and decisions are reached by consultation. The leader's job is to embody the collective will—and feeling insufficiently consulted is a common cause of disagreement. Team members expect to be consulted and to influence the outcome. However, be wary—when things go wrong there can be a tendency

to blame individuals rather than accept collective responsibility.

It is not a good idea to put pressure on people: it tends to have the reverse effect and even slow things down.

BUSINESS ENTERTAINING

Entertaining and socializing are very much part of business life, and are generally informal in style: visitors are as likely to be entertained to lunch in a pub or in the canteen as in a restaurant. Lunch is usually taken at 12:30 or 1:00 p.m.

The ability to relax and enjoy whatever entertainment is provided is important. Join in and treat your hosts as friends: ostentatious self-importance will be considered insulting. A visiting businessman may well be taken to a nightclub after dinner where the revelry can continue into the small hours. Pubs where music is performed, especially traditional music, are a common feature of Irish life, and visitors are often taken along.

It is equally likely that you and your spouse will be invited to your host's home, usually at about 7:30 or 8:00 p.m. If you are, take a small

present for the hostess: wine or chocolates.
Dress is usually informal but not overly casual.

It is normal to return hospitality.

Relax with a Song!

Shyness or reticence is understood, but the visitor
who, when invited, can launch into a song or a
ballad from their own culture will certainly be
appreciated. And it will help in establishing a
relaxed personal relationship with your Irish hosts
that will definitely be advantageous when it comes
to business negotiations.

Despite the famous Irish casualness about time,
the old *laissez-faire* attitudes are being squeezed out
of Irish economic life. If your Irish counterparts
are serious about doing business with you they will
be punctual and will expect the same from you.

The English tend not to confirm business
appointments made by telephone, but in Ireland it
is as well to follow up by fax, letter, or e-mail, and
to make a final confirmation by telephone the day
before meeting.

Unless your host specifies casual dress, wear
a suit for a dinner party. Entry to some nightclubs
will be facilitated by wearing a jacket and tie. Some
upmarket restaurants may expect similar attire.

BUSINESS, SHOPPING, AND BANKING HOURS, AND PUBLIC HOLIDAYS

Most businesses in Ireland operate a forty-hour, five-day week.

Shops are generally open from 9:00 or 9:30 a.m. to 5:30 or 6:00 p.m., Monday to Saturday, but quite a number in the smaller towns still close for at least an hour at lunchtime and on one afternoon each week, usually Wednesday or Thursday. This is true of both Northern Ireland and the Republic.

However, in the cities especially, nowadays there are late-opening minisupermarkets catering for people who operate outside conventional working hours, and Sunday opening is becoming reasonably common in the Republic, less so in Northern Ireland.

Banks are open 10:00 a.m. to 4:00 p.m., Monday to Friday, but often stay open to 5:00 p.m. on Thursdays. The Bank of Ireland bureau de change in Westmoreland Street, Dublin, is open 9:00 a.m. to 9:00 p.m., Monday to Saturday.

Public holidays, when most banks and shops shut, are Christmas Day (December 25), Boxing or St. Stephen's Day (December 26), New Year's Day (January 1) St. Patrick's Day (March 17), Good Friday (late March/early April), Easter Monday (late March/early April), the first Monday in May, the first Monday in June, the first Monday in August, and the last Monday in October.

chapter eight

COMMUNICATING

A LOVE OF THE LANGUAGE

A gift of "blarney" is generally supposed to represent the archetypical Irishman's ability to charm, and there is some truth in the stereotype. Verbal fluency is valued in Ireland. It is what "the *craic*" is all about, and the unbroken line of outstanding Irish playwrights from the eighteenth century onward bears witness to the Irish joy in words and discourse.

THE IMPORTANCE OF UNDERSTATEMENT

While picturesque phrases and colorful images may abound, this is counterbalanced by gently ironic understatement. Somebody who is terminally ill might be said to be looking "a bit shook." If someone suggests a "gargle" they mean going for a drink.

This indirectness often represents a delicate linguistic camouflage under which uncomfortable truths can be hinted at, or propositions advanced, with minimal loss of face if rejected. It is important in doing business, especially in rural areas, to be tuned in to these subtleties.

Learn Patience

The Irish love of conversation means it can be a fine test of one's patience to stand in, say, a supermarket line while the checkout girl chatters to the customer ahead of you about their respective families. Look on it as good training for doing business with an Irish countryman!

At a deeper level, beneath the general bonhomie, the Irish are reticent about exposing their innermost feelings. Not as formal as the English in personal relationships, the Irish are unlikely to bare their souls to anybody other than close friends or family.

WATCH OUT FOR GOSSIP!

The small size of Ireland means everybody knows (or thinks they know) everybody else's business. Gossip travels fast! The other side of the coin is that everyone is keen to preserve their privacy. Consequently there often emerges a wonderful contradiction whereby, in trying to preserve their own privacy, people cheerfully add grist to the rumor mills in order to keep the limelight off themselves . . . but like any mill wheel, it just goes round and round!

ACCENT AND IDIOM

Despite its small population, there is a great deal of regional variation in Ireland, in both accent and phrasing. Dublin people have a famous nasal twang, while the Cork accent is notoriously singsong, and the western soft and gentle. The two communities in the North can be distinguished by the expressions they use and by accent even in the hurly-burly of Belfast City.

Beware of Stereotypes

Cheery Hollywood stereotypes who utter phrases like "top of the morning" (which nobody actually says in Ireland!), can be dangerously misleading, and visitors who put on fake Irish accents are not appreciated.

Although comparatively few Irish people speak Gaelic fluently, many Irish turns of phrase derive from Gaelic usage. Irish has a tense called "the present habitual" and Irish people use what seems to be the present tense where English or Americans would use the past. Irish is a language full of picturesque turns of phrase. You do not wish someone a "Prosperous New Year," but *Go meadai Dia do stor san Athbhliain* ("Goh MAY-dy jeer doh storr sun ACH-vlian")—"May God increase your store of treasure in the New Year!"—and this quality enriches Irish English speech as Synge and O'Casey record in their plays.

Despite these quirks of language, anyone proficient in English should have little difficulty in understanding what is said.

THE MEDIA

Irish Newspapers

Ireland is well provided with newspapers, which have a good mix of national and international news. The *Irish Times*, regarded as the flagship quality daily (though the *Irish Independent* has a larger circulation), is transmitted daily on the Internet.

British newspapers are available throughout Ireland from early on the day of issue. The British tabloids print Irish editions—sometimes with hilarious results, as when anti-Irish headlines are muted or even reversed for these editions.

Partisan Reporting

Belfast papers can be quite sectarian in their reporting. When a drunk was run over on the train track a Republican newspaper was supposedly said to have run the headline "Catholic Killed by Government Train!"

TV and Radio

Eire's publicly-funded TV and radio network, RTE (*Radio Telefis Eirann*: "RAD-io TEL-e-FEES AIR-un") has two English-language television channels, RTE1 and Network 2, and an Irish-language channel, TG4. All carry commercials, but there is also an independent commercial station, TV3. There are three English-language RTE radio networks: Radio 1, Radio 2, and the classical music station Lyric FM; plus Radio Ireland, the Irish-language *Radio na Gaeltachta*, and numerous local stations. BBC radio and TV are easily obtainable in the east, and an extensive cable network distributes four British television channels and twelve satellite channels throughout much of the country. This penetration will increase when a microwave system extends this service to rural areas. RTE gets a respectable 46 percent of the total audience but still has difficulty funding its large commitments.

Northern Ireland has the BBC radio and TV channels plus the commercial Ulster Television, over half of whose viewers are in the Republic. There are a number of local radio stations.

COMMUNICATING AND GETTING AROUND

Telephone

The Irish telecommunications system is very modern—the international network is 100 percent digital, and the digital mobile phone network serves more than 95 percent of the population. Visiting businesspeople should have no difficulty with laptops or cellular phones (provided they are designed for international use). Americans should be aware that local calls are charged. There are a number of Internet providers.

Unfortunately, because they are used to friendly chatter on the telephone, Irish people are not good with voice mail—if the person they are calling is not there they often simply hang up!

To call a U.K. number from Eire, dial 0044 plus the area code without the 0 in front—thus a

number starting 081 would be 0044 81. To call
Northern Ireland, dial 08 then the area code
without dropping the 0. To call elsewhere, dial 00
then the area code for that country. Thus the
U.S.A. is 001. The Northern Ireland service is the
same as that of the rest of the U.K., and calls to
the Republic count as international calls.

Rail and Bus
The Eire Rail network
connects the main towns
and cities. Lines run
from Dublin to Sligo,
and Ballina in the
north, Westport,
Galway, Tralee, and
Ennis in the west, and

Cork, Rosslare, and Bridgetown in the
south. Rail is a fast, cheap, and reliable way of
getting around (though not to more remote
locations), and there are express trains to
Belfast (the "Enterprise" takes two hours).
Dublin has its own metropolitan railway,
the DART.

Northern Ireland is poorly served by rail, but
there is a route to Londonderry from Belfast,
and a couple of other shorter routes.

The bus service, too, can be useful.
Foreigners puzzled by the seemingly ubiquitous

destination *An Lar* (pronounced as written) on Dublin buses should know that it is the Irish for "city center"). And in this respect Northern Ireland is well provided for, with an efficient and wide-ranging bus network.

For those with deeper pockets, it is possible to get around the country by both plane and helicopter, using the regional airports of Donegal, Galway, Kerry, Sligo, Waterford, and Derry.

Roads

The Irish drive on the left as in Britain. Northern Ireland has two motorways, and Dublin has a good ring road. Nowadays there are reasonable roads throughout Ireland thanks to major subsidies from the EU. Generally Irish roads are delightfully uncluttered, but be prepared to be held up by slow agricultural vehicles or even herds of sheep and cattle.

Taxis

Irish taxis can be a means, not only of transport, but of education. For many visitors on their way in from the airport, the taxi driver will be

their first encounter with the irreverent, opinionated, garrulous Dubliner. If you wish to sit stiffly, shrouding yourself in executive privilege, he will not mind, but you may be the loser.

How to Find a Cab

Taxis in urban areas operate from ranks or by telephone call: they do not cruise the streets, as in New York or London.

Because of the cost of cars, hiring a car in Ireland is expensive by British or American standards.

CONCLUSION

The best thing that visitors to Ireland can do is relax and be themselves. You cannot become Irish by a process of osmosis (though some people try!) and no one is expected to master all the subtleties of the local culture. The foreigner in Ireland has a general dispensation to be different. But this book will have given you some idea of what makes the Irish tick: how they conduct business, how they spend their leisure, what they eat and drink, and, above all, what is so special about Ireland. How a hospitable and creative, small island people have had such an impact on the world, and created a culture and literature of which a nation twenty times their size would be proud. And, of course, how they have been shaped by their geography and their history—and maybe why some of them chose not to go West and seek their fortunes in the U.S.A.!

Appendix: Some Famous Irish Americans

Ten Presidents of the United States had Irish roots: Andrew Jackson, James K. Polk, James Buchanan, Ulysses S. Grant, William McKinley, Woodrow Wilson, John Fitzgerald Kennedy, Richard Milhous Nixon, Ronald Reagan, Bill Clinton.

Two signatories of the Declaration of Independence were actually born in Ireland: George Taylor and Matthew Thornton.

Other signatories with Irish roots: Thomas Lynch, Thomas McLean, George Read, Edward Rutledge, James Smith, and Charles Carroll, the only Catholic to sign.

Other notable Irish-Americans: Daniel Boone and Davy Crockett, frontiersmen; Buffalo Bill Cody, showman and frontier scout; Bat Masterson, gunfighter; John O'Hara, Scott Fitzgerald, and Eugene O'Neill, writers; Henry Ford, automobile manufacturer; John Ford, filmmaker; James Cagney, Jackie Gleason, Buster Keaton, Gene Kelly, Grace Kelly, Bing Crosby, and Gregory Peck, actors; Stephen Foster, songwriter; Randolph Hearst, newspaper owner; Ed Murrow, CBS correspondent; John McEnroe, tennis player; John McCloskey, first American cardinal of the Catholic Church; and William J. Brennan and Sandra Day O'Connor, Supreme Court justices.

Further Reading

Beckett, J. C. *The Making of Modern Ireland.*
New York: Alfred A Knopf, 1972.

Cahill, Thomas. *How the Irish Saved Civilization.*
New York: Anchor Books, 1995.

Callan, Lou, et al. *Lonely Planet: Ireland.*
Melbourne/Oakland/London/Paris: Lonely Planet Publications, 2002.

Connolly, S. J. *The Oxford Companion to Irish History.* Oxford: OUP, 1998.

Greenwood, Margaret, et al. *The Rough Guide to Ireland.*
London: Rough Guides, 2001.

Haughton, J. P. (ed.). *Atlas of Ireland.* Dublin: Royal Irish Academy, 1979.

Joyce, J. *Ulysses.* New York: Random House, 1934.

Kennedy & Gillispie (eds.). *Ireland: Art into History.*
Dublin: Townhouse, 1994.

Longley, Michael (ed.) *20th Century Irish Poems.* London: Faber, 2002.

McCourt, Frank. *Angela's Ashes.* London: Flamingo, 1997.

McGahern, John. *That They May Face the Rising Sun.* London: Faber, 2001.

Montague, John (ed). *The Faber Book of Irish Verse.*
London: Faber and Faber, 1974.

Moody, T. W. & Martin, F. X. *The Course of Irish History.*
Dublin: Mercier Press, 1994.

O'Brien, Flann. *The Third Policeman.*
New York: New American Library, 1986.

Synge, J. M. *The Aran Islands.* Oxford: OUP, 1990.

Vallely, Fintan. *Companion to Irish Traditional Music.*
Cork: Cork University Press, 1998.

Yeats, W. B. *Poems, Selected by Seamus Heaney.* London: Faber, 2002.

Index